SOCIAL LIFE IN ANCIENT KASHMIR

SOCIAL LIFE IN ANCIENT KASHMIR

By

Dr. M. Yaqoob Allie

Lecturer in History

Govt. Higher Secondary School, Izmarg

Gurez (Jammu and Kashmir)

(India)

DPH

DISCOVERY PUBLISHING HOUSE PVT. LTD.

INDIA

Published by:
Namit Wasan
DISCOVERY PUBLISHING HOUSE PVT. LTD.
4383/4B, Ansari Road, Darya Ganj
New Delhi-110 002 (India)
Phone : +91-11-23279245; 23253475; 43596065
E-mail : discoverybooksindia@gmail.com
discoverypublishinghouse@gmail.com
namitwasan9@gmail.com
web : www.discoverypublishinggroup.com

First Edition: **2019**

ISBN: 978-93-88854-12-2

Social Life in Ancient Kashmir

Printed at:
Infinity Imaging Systems
Delhi

Dedicated
To
My Parents

Preface

Kashmir is known as the paradise on earth. It has been acclaimed as a land of bless, peace and contentment. The valley is enclosed from all sides by the snow capped mountains, which have provided it with natural protection and have a great bearing on its history. The oval shaped valley is a land of springs, lakes, streams, rivers, fields, forests, and flowers. Kashmir has everything that can stimulate a creative mind and a compelling passion. There is a lot of variety in which there is something for every body's interest. It has scenic beauty for artists, high mountains for mountaineers and other adventure and places suited for specialized sports and everything that can stimulate the creative genius and the art. A meeting place of three great cultures- Hindu, Muslim, and Buddhist. The lovely people of this land have been known for their arts and crafts throughout the world. The soil in the valley is fertile, its climate a temperate and forests are rich. Kashmir is the most beautiful place on earth. Kashmir has remained the home of learning and creative art and literature, from ancient times it has contributed to the growth of philosophy, sciences, language, literature and discourses in religion. Within the whole of South Asia Kashmir is the only region that can claim the distinction of possesses an uninterrupted series of written records of its history and culture.

An endeavour has been made in the present work to give an authentic, impartial and realistic picture of social life in ancient Kashmir. The information for this work has been derived from, literary works, epigraphical evidence, sculptural and archaeological data, and accounts of foreign travellers and historians. The vast amount of literature in Sanskrit written during this period is a mine of information regarding the life and culture of the people. The accounts of foreign pilgrims and travellers have been fully utilised. Information derived from the archaeological material, consisting chiefly of epigraphic records, architectural remains and sculptural antiquities is extremely useful because it is assignable to a particular date or period and is thus more useful than the information derived from literary sources. Evidences from these diverse sources have been properly evaluated, no partiality being shown or undue importance being attached to any one of them. Every care has been taken to check and verify the conclusions based on the data from one of the above sources by considering what other sources have to say on the points concerned.

At the end it is my pleasant duty to express my gratitude to persons from whom I have received valuable help in the completion of the present work. Possibly words may limit my expression I have for my supervisor professor Susmita Pande, whose judicious help and inspiration rendered the present work possible. I would like to be silent to make my debt of gratitude to her more eloquent.

I am immensely grateful to professor Ram Kumar Ahariwar, Dr. Dhirendra Solanki and Dr.Viswajeet Singh Parmar for their kind help, guidance, cooperation and their valuable suggestions, which kept me always on the right track with infinite patience.

I am specially thankful to Dr. Shabir Gassi, Dr. Khursheed padroo, Dr. John paul, Nissar Kumar, Farooq Ganie, and Khan Sajad, through their constrictive criticism and moral support have helped in completing this task.

I do not have adequate words to express what I owe to my colleagues, Sajad Ahmad lone, Khursheed Ahmad, Kaisar Ahmad Malla, Nissar Ahmad, Mohd Asif and Gh. Mohd. Mir. I also acknowledge the instant help rendered by the libraries of, Iqbal library Kashmir University, district library Anantnag, SPS, museum Srinagar, central library university of Jammu, Srinagar archives, library of department of history Vikram university Ujjain, central library Vikram university Ujjain.

Finally, I will be falling in my duties if I do not mention the help I received from my wife Yasmeena who has been a constant source of encouragement for the completion of this work. She always stood by me through my protracted trial.

M. Yaqoob Allie
Lecturer in History
Govt. Higher Secondary School
Izmarg, Gurez

Contents

1

Introduction

Such is Kashmir, the country which may be conquered by the force of spiritual merit but not by armed force; where the inhabitants in consequence fear more the next world; where there are hot baths in winter, comfortable landing places on the river-banks, where the rivers being free from aquatic animals are without peril; where realising that the land created by his father is unable with softness even in summer. Learning, high dwelling houses, saffron, iced water, grapes and the like– what is a commonplace there, is difficult to secure in paradise.

—*Rajatarangini*

Nature itself when creating the great valley of Kashmir and its enclosing wall of mountains seems to have assured to this territory not only a distinct geographical character, but also a historical existence of marked individuality[1].

Kashmir- "The Paradise on Earth" is the nature's gift and the cynosure of all eyes, throughout global.[2] The Kashmir valley ($33^0\ 25'\ 00'$ to $34^0\ 39'\ 30''$ N and $73^0\ 55'\ 05''$ to $75^0\ 36'\ 30''$ E) lies towards the north-west of peninsular India. It is an Oval shaped valley surrounded by chains of mountains which are also oval[3]. The valley has an elevation between 5200 ft. to 6000 ft. above the sea level[4]. The mountains which surround it vary between 12000 ft. to 18000 ft. in height[5]. The flat part of the country is 84 miles long and 20-25 miles broad[6]. The valley of Kashmir has the natural protection of lofty mountains which encircle it[7]. The mountains consist of three main ranges[8], (1) Northern and Eastern Ranges of Nanga Parbat 26620 ft. in the north[9] (2) Harmukh 16903 ft. in the East[10] and (3) Panjal Range 15000 ft. In the south west[11]. The Jhelum or Vihat known as *Vitasta* in Sanskrit is the chief river of Kashmir. The River Jhelum flows from its South-east and goes towards North-west to Baramullah. The river is navigable all through the valley and is a great highway between Kanebal and Srinagar[12]. The river Jhelum fed with large number of tributaries has changed the physical features of the land. There has been extensive dissection of *Karewa* beds, formation of terraces, low land swampy areas and lakes such as Wular, Mansbal, Anchar, Dal, Haigam, Hokersar, besides mountainous lakes like Gangabal, Sheshnag, Tarsar and Marsar, Kounsarnag, Alpather, Butapathri, Nialang, Narannag etc.[13] The valley is gifted with such rare natural scenic beauty that it has been called virtually a heaven on earth.

Kashmir is an ancient land mentioned in the Greek classics of Ptolemy, Dionysios, Hekataios and Helodotos[14]. Hekataeius[15] mentions the city of Kaspatyarus, situated where the Indus becomes navigable, and Kaspapyros as a tribe living on the banks of Indus. Herodotus mention Kashmir by the name of Kaspatyros[16]. Dionysios mentions the Kaspeiroi as a tribe famous among all Indians for their fast feet[17].

The Chinese have referred to Kashmir and there are clear references to the valley in the Annals of the Tang dynasty[18]. Hiuen- Tsang, who visited valley in 631A.D. and stayed there as an honoured guest for fully two years[19], his description of the kingdom *"Kih- Shi- mi- Lo"* shows clearly that Kashmir must have been restricted to the great basin of *Vitasta* and the side valleys drained by its tributaries above the Baramula defile. He observes that the valley is surrounded on all sides by mountains which are very high. Although the mountains have passes through them, these are narrow and contracted[20]. Though the climate is cold and the snow plentiful, the soil is described as fertile and abounding with fruits and flowers[21]. He speaks of Kashmiri's as handsome, learned, frivolous and clever. Chinese call Kashmir Ki-Pin, while Tibetans call

Kashmir Khe- Che- Yul or Kha- Chhul, and its natives Kha-Chhe-Pa[22]. Kashmir is known to its inhabitants as Kashir[23].

Kashmir is surrounded by a grit of mountains, which is crosses through a few mountain passes. Ou- Kong has described the three passes leading to the valley. One pass leads from Tou- fan (Tibet); the other from Po-Liu (Baltistan) and the third from Kien- To-Lo (Gandhara)[24]. It is evident that Kashmir had established links with the people of Ladakh, Tibet, Gilgit, Taxila and Peshawar from earliest times[25].

According to the *Nilamatapurana*[26], Kashmir was once a vast lake called Satisara. In which Goddess Parvati sailed in a pleasure boat. But it was occupied by a demon called Jalodbhava (water- born), who destroyed all life in the lake and rendered the country waste. In the 7th Manvantra the water of the lake was drained off by Ananta, at the behest of Vishnu, through any outlet at Baramulla. The chief of the Nagas, the author of the *Purana* and the son of sage Kashyapa, took care of the land and the valley came to known as Kashafmar, home of Kashyapa and is now corrupted to Kashmir[27]. The same legend about the draining off the lake also occurs in Kalhana's *Rajatarangini*. He says that Prajapati Kashyapa was assisted by Brahma, Vishnu and Shiva in killing the demon of lake, Jalodbhava. After his death, the lake water was drained off and the land came to be known as Kashmir after Kashyapa.[28]

The *Nilamata* informs us that the valley of Kashmir called Satidesa was occupied in ancient times by the Nagas only.[29] According to Kalhana Nagas were the aborigines of the valley, they were tribal people and snake worshippers.[30] Afterwards the Pisacas and the descendants of Manu also became their cohabitants.[31] They are said to have close association with the people living in the neighbouring countries. They used to go to these countries periodically and return to the valley whenever the climatic conditions were favourable. In this way, despite mountainous barriers, there was continuous movement of the people coming into and leaving out of the valley. Both the tribes inhabited the valley on different occasions. The Nagas lived during summer months and the Pisachas occupied it in winter season.[32] Then came the Aryan invasion from the north-west of India. That was about 3000 years ago. The Aryans coming via Gilgit and Chitral mixed with the aborigines.

The first king who is mentioned in Kalhan's chronicle by name is Gonanda I[33], whose initial year of reign places in 653 Kali, the traditional date of the coronation of king Yudhisthira the Pandava leader. Gonanda I went to war with lord Krishna, on behalf of his relative Jarasandha, king of Magada, and laid siege to the town of Mathura, but was defeated and killed[34]. He was succeeded by his son Damodra I[35] who, impelled by the desire to avenge his father's death, attacked Krishna. He too was killed were upon Krishna installed the late Kings pregnant widow, Yasovati, on the throne[36]. The Queen gave birth to a son who was placed on the throne as Gonanda-II.[37] Gonanda II was followed by 35 kings whose names perished through the destruction of records[38]. They were followed by eight kings named respectively as lava, Kusa, Khanendra, Surendra, Godhara, Suvarha, Janaka and Sacinara[39]. The first four belonged to one dynasty and the last four to the other. It is said that some of these princess granted *Agraharas* to the Brahmans, a few of them built towns and one of them excavated a camel.[40] But nothing is known about the historicity of any of them.[41]

The next king mentioned is Ashoka.[42] Kalhana supplies an erroneous pedigree to Ashoka as he called him a great-grandson of Sakuni.[43] Ashoka's was the first secular welfare state. According to *Mahavamsa*, Ashoka's adviser, Moggaliputta Tissa sent his missionary Majjhantika to peach Buddhism in Kashmir and Gandhara[44]. Ashoka not only sent missionaries to propagate Buddhism in Kashmir, but built there numerous *Stupas* and *Viharas* as well[45]. The introduction of Buddhism in Kashmir by king Ashoka marks the watershed in the religious history of Kashmir. With the advent of Buddhism, Kashmir became a part of wider Buddhist world and this enabled a steady exchange of ideas and influences between Kashmir and rest of Buddhist India. Kalhana who was himself a Shaiva has recorded that during the period of Ashoka a Shiva temple of *Vijayeshvara* was repaired and two new ones called *Ashokesvara* were built by him.[46] He acted on the policy of religious toleration and patronized all religions.

The important contribution of King Ashoka was that he built the original city of Shrinagari[47], identified at a about four miles above the existing capital which is now occupied by a small village of Pandrethan (Kalhana's Puranadhisthana) which required the capital of Ancient Kashmir till the end of 6th century. When the capital was shifted further down to the area known as "Pravarasenapurea" (Modern Srinagar) which continues to be so even now.[48] Ashoka had broken through the fetter of Brahmanism and established friendly intercourse with Greece and Egypt, and it is to this connection that the introduction of stones architecture and sculpture in Kashmir is due.

If Kalhana is to be believed, Ashoka was succeeded on the throne of this northernmost territory by his son Jalauka[49]. He is described as a great warrior who cleared the land of oppressing *Mlecchas* and affected extensive conquests, including Kanyakubja[50]. From the subdued regions he is supposed to have brought settlers to Kashmir, people of all castes particularly righteous men acquainted with legal procedure[51]. Jalauka, was a popular hero and a worshiper of Shiva. He and made a vow that he would ever worship Shiva *Vijayesvara* and *Jyesthesa* residing at Nadisaksetra[52]. The first religious edifice on the isolated hill, rising to about 1000 feet above the plains, and known as Takth-i-Sulaiman and called by Hindus Cankaracharya, was built by Jaloka about 200 BC.[53] It is said that he was not favourable to Buddhism in the beginning[54], but subsequently at the request of Kritya he modified his attitude and built one Buddhist *Vihara*, named Krityasrama[55]. Jalauka was succeeded by Damodara-II, who was either descended from the house of Ashok or was born in some other dynasty, protected the land as King[56]. He built a town on the Damodra-suda (Modern Damodar Udar), round and arid alluvial plateau to the south of Srinagar[57]. As apparent from the account Kalhana, Damodara-II, too was a devout Shaiva like Jalauka and he also understood certain constructions for proving irrigational facilities for his subjects[58].

After he passed away Kashmir is said to have come under the Kushana occupation. According to Kalhana, among the Kushana enters whose sway extended to Kashmir included Huska, Juska and Kanisha[59]. Each one of them founded here a town after his name, and these were called Huskapura; Juskapura and Kaniskapura respectively[60].

The Kushana Empire reached the Pinnacle of its glory under the patronage of his successor–Kanishka (123-153 AD)[61]. Kanishka conquered the whole of north India, from Kashmir to Ujjain. Thus he became the ruler of a vast Kushana empire, which included ancient Bactria besides the vast regions of Kabul, Gandhara, Kashmir, Punjab, Taxila, Mathura, Ujjain and Patliputra. Besides being a great conqueror Kanishka is known to have been a liberal patron of arts and letters. His court was adorned by some of the greatest intellects of the age. Among these were the celebrated Sanskrit poet, dramatist and musician, Ashvghosha and scholars Parshva, Vasumitra and Sangha-rakhaha. His physician Charaka-the father of Indian medicine was a Kashmiri[62]. According to the Buddhist tradition, Kanishka held the fourth Buddhist Council in Kashmir.[63] In which the majority of the participants were Sarvastivadins. The object of the council was to prepare commentaries on the Canons. Since he was upset with growing controversies and conflicting interpretation of Buddha's words. The commentaries called *Vibhashas* were written on Sanskrit language. The treaties written on copper plates had been enclosed in stone boxes and deposited in a *Stupa* made especially for the purpose[64].

After the Kushanas, the fearless Abhimanyu, who knew no foes (*kantaka*), and was like Indra (*Satamanyu*), became king[65].The king was a great supporter of Shaivism and promoter of Sanskrit learning. He founded the city of

Abhimanyupura[66]. Candracarya and others on his instructions brought the *Mahabhasya* in Kashmir.[67] During this era the power of the Buddhists whom the wise Bodhisattva Nagarjuna had protected predominated in the land[68]. It seems the Nagas were offended at this development and came in conflict, perhaps bloody, with the Buddhists who suffered greatly, consequently[69]. The Naga cult was restored by a Brahman, Chandradeva[70].

Abhimanyu's was succeeded by Gonanda-III who was a very pious and religious minded king[71]. He further promoted the cause of the traditional religion. Gonanda III was succeeded by several princesses of whom we have only recorded the dry list of names and the duration of their reigns. These were Vibhishana, who reigned 53 years, Inderjita 35 years and 6 month, Ravana 30 years, Vibhishana II 35 years and 6 months meaning an aggregate of 154 years[72] of Ravana, it is said that he extended the worship of Shiva as the Linga Vateshwara and of the second Vibishana that he was both a patron and cultivator of the art of music, the Muhammadan writers say, that in these days Tiranahs ascribed to this prince were current in Kashmir.[73] Vibhishana II was followed by Nara, who was also known as Kimnara[74]. He levelled the Buddhist temples to the ground[75], burnt thousands of *Viharas*, and confiscated Buddhist lands[76]. He built a city on the sandy banks of the *Vitasta*, where the markets were kept full of supplies by the highroads leading to it, and where the coming and going of ships gave splendour to the river.[77] After Nara, the valley witnessed the reign of many kings like Siddha[78], Utpalaksha[79], Hiranyaksha[80] and Vasukula[81] who like their predecessors were non-descript.

The next important king mentioned by Kalhana is Mihirakula.[82] He was cruel, ruthless and anti Buddhist. Kalhana who places him about twelve hundred years before his time describes him as the enemy of mankind, with no pity for children, compassion for women or respect for the aged, whose approach the people knew "by noticing the vultures, crows, and other birds which were flying ahead eager to feed on those who were to be"[83]. Kalhana's description of Mihirakula as rapacious and blood thirsty receives corroboration from Hiuen Tsang's account. Hence in general were responsible for the wholesale destruction of Buddhist monasteries. On the other hand, Mihirkula was a devotee of Shiva. He is said to have built a shrine of Shiva at Srinagar, and founded the town Mihirapura and donated *agraharas* to Ganghara Brahmans[84]. A number of Brahmans belonging to the Gandhara region were invited to settle down in Kashmir and received land grants from him.[85] The king ended his life by throwing himself into fire[86].

Mihirkula was succeeded by his son Baka.[87] He constructed the temple of Shiva Bakesa, founded the city called Lavanotsa and caused the Bakavait canal to be dug out all in public interest.[88] The king passed sixty three years and thirteen days as ruler of valley.[89] Baka was followed by four kings, Kshitivanda, Vasunanda, Nara II, Aksa and Gopaditya. Vaunanda, composed a well known work on erotic's (*Smarasasrta*)[90]. King founded the village of Aksavala[91]. He established the *Agraharas* bearing the names of *Khola, Khagika, Hadigrama* and *Skandapura*, as well as the *agraharas* of *Samajasa* and others[92]. Gopaditya is credited to have established the temple of Jyesthesvara on the Gopa hill. He donated land to Brahmins from Aryadesha near its vicinity[93]. He stopped the slaughter of animals.[94] Gokarna, his son established the temple of Shiva Gokaranesvara, he ruled for fifty – seven years and nine months.[95]

He was succeeded by his son Narendraditya-i alias Khinkhila[96]. He was the founder of the temple of Bhutesvara and of a hospice[97]. He ruled for thirty- six years and a hundred days[98].

He was followed by Yudhisthira-i better known as Andha-Yudhisthira (the blind Yudhisthira).[99] He was an oppressive ruler and was forced to flee the country by his ministers and subjects[100]. After Yudhisthira's dethronement, the nobles of Kashmir Invited from India a relative of king Vikramaditya of India and crowned him as king of Kashmir under the name of Pratapaditya.[101] The valley from the time of Pratapaditya onwards suffered from internal dissensions and consequently became subject to Harsha and other foreigners.[102] After the reign of thirty-two years his son Jakukas became the ruler of valley[103]. Then his son Tonjina along with his queen Vakpusta ruled the valley[104]. According to Kalhana, Tunjina and his pious wife Vakpusta built the temple of Shiva called Tungesvara, a graceful embellishment of the earth, as well as the town Katika[105]. Tunjina was a contemporary of great poet Candka.[106] Tanjina left no son and another unknown family than occupied the throne. Vijaya, the first king of this time, built the shrine of Vijayesvara[107]. He was followed by his son Jayendra and the later by his minister Samdhimati.[108] Samadhimati was a pious ruler. He was great devotee of Shiva and therefore Shavism gained considerable ground in Kashmir. He built shrines of Siva, and founded lingas, trisulas and bulls of Siva[109]. But his pacifism was disliked by the people, who compelled him to retire and brought in place Meghavahana.[110]

Meghavahana who was living in exile at the Gandhara court when the Kashmir throne fell vacant was approached by the Kashmiri ministers to occupy it. This he willingly did. He is said to have been a kind hearted man and prohibited the slaughter of animals even in sacrificial throughout the realm. The prohibition was later extended to the killing of birds and fishes also[111]. In fact he was so keen about the practice of non violence that he is represented as having undertaken a *digvijaya*[112]. Meghavahana the city of *Mayustagrama*, established the *agrahara* called *Meghavana* and built a convent after his name[113]. The king's wife Amritaprabha, built a lofty *Vihara* known as Amritabhanana for the benefit of foreign Bhikahus (monks)[114]. His guru who hailed from Loh (leh) built the magnificent Stupa known as Lo-stonpa[115]. His queen Yukadevi built a *Vihara* of wonderful appearance at Nadavava (Narvor) in the northern part of Srinagar[116]. Bachelors and married Bhikshus both were accommodated in it. Then another wife of the king, called

Indradevi built a *Vihara* called Indradevibhavana and also built a *Stupa*[117]. Kalhana credits his reign for considerable building activities on the part of his numerous queens and also for his victories over many kings and territories as for Srilanka, which is quite incredible though he might have had Bhikshus from that county and this gesture was subsequently interpreted as conquest. He was succeeded by his son Sreshtasena. He was also known by the names of Pravarasena-I and Tunjana-II[118]. Pravarasena-i was himself a great builder. He erected many sacred buildings at Purandisthana.[119]. He was succeeded by his two sons, Hiranya and Toramana, the former occupied the throne, and later being styled as Yuvaraja[120]. Once Toramana coined money in his own name, this incited the wrath of Hiranya who put the later into prison[121]. Shortly after he was set free by his brother, Toramana died. At the same time Hiranya died without heir and the throne of Kashmir which fell vacant was filled up by a poet named Matrgupta, a nominee of king Vikramaditya of Ujjain. This poet king was patron of literature and Viashnava in faith. He extended his patronage to Bhartrinantha and built a shrine of Vishnu. Matragupta Svamina.[122] After Matragupta, PravarasenaII seized the throne of Kashmir. Pravarasena-II laid the foundation of new city called "Pravarasenapura" northwest of the old capital of Ashoka's Purranadhisthana. The new capital is identified as the present capital, Srinagar.[123], to which he transferred his capital from Srinagar founded by Ashoka. In the new town which lay between the right bank of *Vitasta* and the foot of the Hari Parbat hill, he erected a number of palatial buildings and temples. The massive ruins of some of these can be seen to this day outside the high wall which surrounded the hill on its south-west. The successor of this prince was his son Yudishtir, who reigned thirty nine years and three months. He was succeeded by his younger brother Lakhana Narendraditya, he founded Narendrasvamin.[124] He founded an office of state for the preservation of written records.[125]

Ramaditya was the next king. He was so much solicitors of the warfare of his subjects that, besides other buildings, he established a faultless hospital for the healing of sick people. He is also said to have married a Chola princess named Penarambhal. The last king of this dynasty was Baladitya. After him ascended on the throne of Kashmir the well known Karkota Dynasty came.[126]

The Karkota Dynasty was founded in 627A.D. by king Durlbabhvarndhana[127]. With Durlabhavradhana we enter the Golden age of Kashmir's long and chequered history. Kalhan's history assumes an authentic character and gives more detailed and reliable information about the dynasties ruled from the seventh century CE to his own Times (1149AD). From here onwards we can check the majority of the recorded royal names from coins or foreign notices and the chronology too becomes within certain limits, reliable.[128] Durlabhvardhana has his descent from Karkota Naga of the valley and hence the dynasty of which he said the foundation is named as the Karkota Dynasty.[129] His reign is important in the Buddhist history of Kashmir as it was then that Hiuen Tsang is believed to have visited the valley. The celebrated Chinese Scholar who lived as an honoured guest in the valley for two years has left an interesting account of the Kashmir of his time[130]. In Kashmir Hiuen Tsang studied the various sutras and shastras and visited the various Buddhist monasteries and *stupas* to pay his homage to the relics enshrined there. He saw at the time of his stay in Kashmir, one hundred Buddhist monasteries with five thousand Buddhist priests. The Chinese scholar found Kashmir peaceful and prosperous. Learning was held high esteem in the country. After Durlabhavardhana's death his son pratapaditya-II Durlabhaka became king[131]. He seems to have had a long but uneventful reign. He laid the foundation of the town which he named after him and is known as Pratapaditya (Tapar)[132]. Durlabhaka married a lady Narendraprabha, the beautiful wife of Nora, a merchant of Rauhitaka country and from her had three sons Chandrapida, Tarapida and Muktapida.[133] The princes were also known as Vajraditya, Udayaditya and Lalitaditya.

Chindrapida, the eldest son succeeded his father Pratapaditya II.[134] Kalhan mention him as 'Crest-Jewel' among the kings which indicate that he was a man of noble character and high administrative skills.[135] He is also mentioned in the Chinese annals as *Tchen-to-lo-pi-li*.[136] Chandrapida is known for his justice and in his time even the highest could not escape punishment for their misdeed. Chandrapida was succeeded by the cruel ruler Tarapida[137], who created terror by his glory in the valley. Thereafter the throne of Kashmir passed into the hands of Lalitaditaya, the greatest of Kashmir's indigenous rulers[138].

Lalitaditya ascended the throne in 724. He is known in the history as great ruler who brought glory and honour to the Kashmiri's. He ushered a new era of prosperity in the realm. He was a great conqueror and the major part of his thirty-six years reign was passed in expeditions abroad. According to the Kalhana the kings eager for conquests, passed his life chiefly on expeditions, moving round the earth like the sun[139]. These conquests extended from Bengal in the east to Kathiawar in the west and from Malabar in the south to the central Asian deserts in the north. His most notable victory in India was achieved against Yashovarman of Kanauj who was then the most powerful ruler in northern India[140]. After subduing the kings of India he turned his attention to central Asia and everywhere victorious returned after twelve years, to Kashmir by way of Tibet. In the north Lalitaditya succeeded in subjugating a number of territories, including Kamboja (eastern Afghanistan), Tukharistan, Ladakh, the land of the Bhauttas and Dardistan, including Gilgit[141]. From the conquered territories he brought with him learned men and skilled artisans who were appointed to high offices[142]. He raised his country to a pitch of glory it had never reached before. The ruins of the temple of Martand and of his city Parihasapura, bear the testimony of his greatness.

This was a major period of building activities accomplished mainly due to the wealth and power of the monarch. He ushered in a new memorable period not only in the history of Kashmir but also in that of whole of India[143]. The vast treasures which he had brought from the subdued regions were spent in the building of new towns and splendid edifices. The foremost among all his foundations was the new capital Parihasapora[144] near the confluence of the *Vitasta* and the Sindh, about a dozen miles from Srinagar[145]. Lalitaditya like his ancestors was himself a devotee of Vishnu. But he patronised all faiths equally. Here in the temple of Muktakesava, he kept a golden image of Vishnu, in the temple of Parihaskesava, an image of Vishnu made of silver, in the Mahavaraha temple, the image of Vishnu clad in golden armour and then again the silver image of Vishnu was installed in the temple of Goverdhanadhara[146]. In this town the great king erected some of the most magnificent buildings ever built in Kashmir.

Lalitaditya is famous for the sun temple which he built at of Martand (present Mattan about five miles from Anantnag)[147]. The remains of Martand temple are still the most striking object of ancient Hindu architecture in the valley[148]. No temple was ever built on finer site. It stands on an open plain, where it can seen to full advantage. Behind it raises a range of snowy mountains. The temple dedicated to Surya occupies a unique position here. Its beauty, magnificence and architectural achievements have struck scholars, art lovers and archaeologists with wonder. The celebrated temple of Martand possesses far more imposing dimensions than any other existing temple, being 63 feet long. The pillared quadrangle round the temple is 220 feet by 142 feet. The stone carving is very fine indeed[149].

At Huskapura this noble minded king built the splendid shine of Vishnu Muktasvamin and a large *Vihara* with a *Stupa*[150]. His minister Kayya built famous Kayyavihara where Bhikshu Sarvajnamitra who had attained the purity of Buddha had lived[151]. His minister Cankuna built Cankunavihara and erected a lofty *stupa*, a beautiful *Vihara* together with a Chaitya and adorned the *Vihara* with a golden image of Buddha. Cankunas son in law Isana Chandra also built a *Vihara*. Cankunavihara[152] in Parihaspura was extant in Kalhana's time.

Lalitaditya was followed by a succession of weak kings who were unable to maintain the power and prestige of the Lalitaditya's vast empire. He was soon followed by his elder son Kuvalayapida[153]. He was a pious king and had no interest in worldly tastes. He is said to have abandoned the throne after one year, and after a life of pious resignation abroad to have attained supernatural perfection[154]. Kuvalayapida was succeeded by his brother Vajraditya also known by the name of Bappiyaka, who was born of Chakramardika, another queen, of Lalitaditya[155]. He is described as a cruel and lustful prince. He is said to have passes his days in the company of large number of women of his seraglio[156]. The wealth and costly articles which his father has collected at his capital Parishapura were taken away and squandered by him.[157] For seven years he led his sensuous life when he succumbed to consumption on by his excesses.[158] Then his son Prthivyapida who was born from queen Manjarika, a destroyer of his subjects became the ruler of valley[159]. He is said to have ruled for four years and one month. He was dethroned by his younger brother, Samgramapida whose reign lasted for only seven days[160].

Jayapida,[161] the youngest son of Vajraditya, who occupied the throne about twelve years after Lalitaditya tried to revive the glorious traditions of his illustrious grandfather. He was good and just ruler and is said to have equated to his grandfather Lalitaditya. He restored peace and order in the state and set up efficient administration. Then he marched for his conquests Kalhana describes that he subjugated all the kingdoms of northern India up to Prayaga[162] (Allahabad). He then left his army in charge of his minister Devasarman and went on an incognito adventure to Bengal where he killed, in a single combat, a dreaded lion. This won him the affection of the ruling chief, Jayanta[163], who gave him his daughter in mirage. Both he and Jayanta then led and army to the neighbouring territories and subjugated the. According to Kalhana he defeated the five Gaudas and the king of Kanauj[164].

Jayapida's building activities deserve a mention. In Srinagar he founded a shrine of Jayadevi, and set up three Buddhist images. He also built a large *Vihara*[165]. Like his grandfather he founded a new town, named after him Jayapura[166]. Inside this town he installed a number of sacred images including that of Buddha. His wives and ministers also erected sacred buildings. Jayadatta, a minister built a Matha in Jayapura[167]. Jayapida was himself a man of great learning extended his patronage to scholars and learned men. He gathered a number of them at his court. It was during his reign probably that Shantiprabha lived in Kashmir along with his disciples Punyakirti, Danshala, Visheshamitra, Prajnavarman and Shura.

The subsequent years after the death of Jayapida ushered in an era of distress, oppression and spirit of self-aggrandisement amongst officers of the state which, unhappily for the people of Kashmir, continued unbridled during the rule of his successors. The Karkotas, who had brought peace and prosperity to that part of country, finished ingloriously. Given to worst human weakness, the subsequent rulers allowed free reins to their officers and favourites with the result that the people were drained dry of all their wealth. There was no security of life and property, the vast dominions, earned at great costs of men and money, had shrunken and the feudal lords as well as enterprising men were strengthening themselves; there was utter disregard of affairs had happenings on the border lands and the pleasure-seeking rulers had no political vision and were impervious towards events of far-reaching consequences happening all round them. Ultimately, the minister Sura was able to seat Avantivarman, grandson of Utpalaka, who, incidentally, was the founder of a new dynasty after the name of his grandfather, in Kashmir.

Avantivarman (855-883A.D.)[168] the son of Sukhavarman ascended the throne in 855A.D., he like Lalityaditya is recorded as a celebrated ruler in the history. With the accession of Avantivarman, we reach that period of Kashmir history for which Kalhan's work presents us with a truly historical record.[169] The use of contemporary accounts from the commencement of his reign onwards becomes evident, not only from the generally Sober and matter-of-fact narrative but also from the use of exact dates.[170] Avantivarman's reign appears to have brought a period of consolidation and prosperity for the kingdom which had suffered considerably from internal troubles during the preceding reigns.[171] He was the noblest of all the rulers of ancient Kashmir. He waged no wars, not even to regain control over the territories which his predecessors had lost not long ago. His were the piping times of peace and plenty, and in point of prosperity, about the quarter of a century of his rule found Kashmir at its zenith. Never before or for centuries later were the people as happy as they were in his time. Truly, therefore, Avantivarman's reign forms a glorious chapter in the history of Kashmir[172]. It is plainly indicated by the large number of temples and endowments, the foundation of which by the pious king and his court Kalhana records in great detail[173]. Foremost among these foundations were the town of Avantipura, an abode of abundant enjoyment[174]. Avantipura stood on the high and dry area of western hills on the right bank of Jhelum (*Vitasta*), 27Kms from Srinagar on the Srinagar-Jammu highway. Owing to its central and strategic location in the valley, the city was of considerable importance since the date of its foundation. According to chronicles of Kalhan, Jona Raja and Srivara, it covered a large area. It was a flourishing city up to the 12th century A.D. when it was destroyed and burnt down by Damaras (Feudal Hindu tribe).[175] He along with his officials and relatives built numerous shrines but at his capital city (Avantipura) his two temples one dedicated to Vishnu called Avantivamin and other to Shiva called Avantishvara are the outstanding works of art and show a considerable advance in sculptured decoration.[176] He also founded the shrines of Tripuresvara, Bhutesa, and Vijayesa.[177]

Both Avantivarma and his minister's were great patrons of learning. A galaxy of poets and scholars adorned his court.

These include the well known Sanskrit poets Shivasvamin, Ratnakara, and Anandavardhana. Their extant works occupy a prominent position in the Sanskrit literature of old Kashmir[178]. There also lived a number of *Siddhas, i.e,* persons who had achieved spiritual perfection.

An achievement of real skill and of a nature that is curiously modern in character was carried out in Avantivarman's reign. This was an engineering feat by which the waters of the Jhelum were diverted and the place of the junction of the Sind River with the Jhelum altered. The person responsible for this task was a man named Suyya. The country had been liable to heavy floods and famines. The Kashmir valley was in a water logged condition. Cultivation was very poor. Avantivarman's able engineer, Suyya undertook to drain the valley.[179] According the price of a *Khari* of rice rose to ten hundred and fifty Dinnars.[180] At that time appeared Suyya. His birth is woven in mystery. When a baby, he had been left by some unfortunate women in a converted earthen pot on the roadside and was picked up by a Chandala, women, and brought up by a Sudra nurse, Suyya, became a teacher of small boys and having, caught the attention of the King and was able to come to the rescue of the people[181]. Suyya insisted that, given an opportunity and means to carry out his scheme, he could relieve the sufferings of the people. Avantivarman was impressed by his confident tone and allowed him for reins to carry out his plan of clearing the *Vitasta* of its boulders. The chronicle has given a graphic account of his schemes. Soon the bed of the river was cleared and a dam constructed for storing its waters for agriculture purposes. Suyya also planned the confluence of Sindhu (Indus) and *Vitasta* (Jhelum) near Srinagar which had their junction near the temple of Vainyasvami. The collected waters of the river were allowed to different villages for irrigational purposes through minor streams and these were rendered safe through embankments constructed at suitable distances[182]. These and food-grain store houses (Kundalas) established at a number of places brought immediate relief to the people who had now more land at their disposal to cultivate with assured supplies of water. Suyya indeed deserve the high praises heaped upon him in the chronicle for his unitising efforts, prices of food-grains, which had rocketed as high as 10.50 Dinars per Khari[183]. Thus the engineering dexterity and genius of Suyya was fully utilised by Avantivarman and the valley was once more on the way of prosperity.

Avantivarman also prohibited the slaughter of animals in his kingdom. His pious engineer Suyya, who was also a Vaishnava, later issued a prohibition against the killing of fishes in the *Vitasta*[184]. Suyya's memory lives in the present Sopore[185], the town he built on the bank of the *Vitasta* just at that point where it leaves the base of the Wular Lake. He granted the village Suyyakundala to the Brahmins in honour of his mother Suyya and constructed the bund Suyya-setu after her name Suyyasetu.[186] On the lands which he raised from the water, thousands of villages such as Jayasthala, etc were founded by Avantivarman and others[187].

The process of disintegration which had started towards the end of Jayapita's reign was barely checked by Avantiavrman. It started once again after his death. Avantivarman died as a devout Vaishnava in 883 A.D. at Tripuresa hill.[188] Soon after his death a civil war began amongst the proud and numerous descendants of Utpala who all aspired each and all to the throne. The Pratihara Ratnavardhana secured by his exertions the kingdom for Sankaravarman, the son of Avantivarman.[189]

Unlike Avantinrman his son did not remain silent but initiated several successful and unsuccessful expeditions to far-flung regions of India and central Asian. He started the expansion with the help of a fantastically large number of forces - nine lakh foot soldiers, one lakh horsemen and three hundred elephants. Kalhan wants us to believe that Samakaravarma faced no difficulty in raising the army even though the country of Kashmir had through the action of time become reduced in population and wealth.[190] The first object of his expedition was the recapture of Darvabhisara, the tract of the lower hills between the Jhelum and Chenab, which had been lost during the unsettled times of the later Karkota Kings. Prithvichandra, the ruler of Trigarta, the present Kangra, who came to offer homage is said to have fled in terror on seeing his immense army.[191]

The main force of Samkaravarman's attack appears to have spent itself in a victory over Alakhana, the ruler of Gujara. This territory, the name of which is preserved in that of the modern town of Gujarat in West Punjab, comprised the upper portion of the land between the Jhelum and the Chenab South of Darvabhisara. Alakhana submitted and ceded a part of his dominions, called Takkadesha, to Samkaravarman.[192] Next, Samkaravarman forced King Bhoja not only to release a scion of the Thakkiya family from his service but also to recognise his independence.[193]

Another expedition which Samkaravarman led to extend his kingdom was against Lalliya whom he desired, "to remove from his sovereign position." But though Kalhan gives details of the campaign, he is cautious regarding the result, which we may assume to have been without any material success of his arms in this direction.[194]

Samkaravarma founded a new city, Shankarapura[195], corresponding to the village Pattan (his capital) on the highway from Srinagar to Baramulla. This is established by Kalhan's testimony, he says that Shanker-Pattan lost its proper appellation and became only known by the name Pattan. So build this city Shankarvarma used the structural material from Lalitaditya's city of Parihaspur[196], which had already suffered on account of the Suyya having removed the confluence of the *Vitasta* and Sindh about two miles away- from Trigrami near Parihasapora to its present site at Shadipore (ancient Shardapora). The capital city was beautiful with the erection of two temples dedicated to Shiva. One was Sugandesha temple built by Queen Sugandha and other, Shankaragaurishvara temple built by the King himself.

Both the temples do not differ from other temples in plan and design,[197] but close investigation reveals that they do not match the grandeur or glory of the earlier structures. Leaving aside the uniformity of the Square Sanctum, with Portico in its front, trefoiled niches surmounted by pediments and the carvings of the repeated patterns or designs like grinning lions heads and human-headed birds observed at both the shrines. One fundamental lacuna is the absence of peristyle at the King's temple of Shahankaragaurishvara. The temple plinth stands exposed but still no trace of the peristyle is forthcoming as was earlier presumed.[198]

Sankaravarman exhausted the royal treasury on military preparations as well as in extravagance[199]. He levied new taxes and did not spare even temples whose main sources of income were charities and public benefactions. The fresh taxes were realised with severe strictness and he also created two new offices – those of Attapatibhaga and Grihakritya for controlling domestic affairs.[200] Even articles like incense, Sandal-wood and other's used in worship were not exempted. Certain extraordinary measures like reduction of weights and measures by 1/3rd were introduced and the masses had to undergo several hardships.[201] Equally oppressive for the cultivators were the excessive demands made for forced labour. Samakaravarma seems to have organised them on a systematic basis and to employ them also as a means for fiscal extortion. Used chiefly for transport purposes, this system of "Begar"[202] has remained a characteristic feature of Kashmir administration up to modern days. Kalhan describes with much bitterness the baneful effects of this regime which favoured only the rapacious tribe of officers (Kayastha) and left men of learning un provided with emoluments.

For over hundred years after Shankaravarman's death Kashmir witnessed misrule of very bad type. The rulers had little use for principles and few scruples. Most of them were dissolute and tyrannical. Apart from indulgence in grossly sensual pleasures their one aim in life was to maintain themselves on the throne as long as they could. Their weak character and wearer administration led to the growth of powerful military clans known as *Tantrin* and *Ekangas*. This latter wielded great power and often the ruler and the councillors were just puppets in their hands. To win the support of these mercenaries no price was considered as too high.

Then Gopalavarman, who excelled in virtue and kept faithful to his engagements, ruled the valley under the guardianship of his mother Sugandha[203]. Queen Sugandha is said to have fell in love with the minister named Prabhakaradeva. She bestowed upon him fortune, rank and love. So he exercised the real powers of the king[204]. Kalhana describes that he bestowed the kingdom of the rebellious Sahi upon Toramana, Lalliya's son, and gave him the new name Kamaluka[205].

Then Gopalavarman's brother Samkata, who had been picked up from the highway, obtained the throne. But he died only after ten days.[206] There upon when king Samkaravarman's lineage had died out, Sugandha had no option except to take the reigns of realm in her own hands[207]. She founded the temple of Gopalapura, the Gopalamatha, the temple of Vishnu Gopalakesava, and another town, Sugandhapura.[208]

Partha, a son of Nirjitavarman the cripple, was placed on the throne when the valley was passing through chaotic conditions.[209] It has been noted that Sugandha, the displaced Queen, made a vain attempt to recapture and put to death by the well organised Tantrins, who also had the support of some court-officials.[210] Henceforth, the valley was subjected to one of the worst kinds of maladministration known in its history. Partha was placed under the regency of his father, Nirjitavarman, as the former was a child.[211] During the reign of Partha the country was a prey to the oppression of tantrins. Niritavarman, became child kings guardian, who became the actual ruler of the valley. He could maintain himself only by paying heavy bribes to the Tantrins, oppressed the people.[212] According to Kalhana, "in this land, the rulers of which had conquered Kanyakubja and other countries, the kings now maintained themselves by giving bills of exchange(hundika) to the Tantrins".[213] The miseries of the masses were further augmented by natural calamities and the valley witnessed one of its worst famines in 917-18 A.D., which carried away a considerable part of population. The prices increased to such an extent that was difficult to obtain food while one khari of rice selling for a thousand dinars.[214] Corpses were thrown into the Jhelum (*Vitasta*) the entire land was laid waste and parched bones covered the open spaces making the country look like a huge burial-ground[215]. The ministers and Tantrins became wealthy, as they amassed riches by selling stores of rice at high prices.[216]

Nirjitavarman, who had played such a nefarious role as regent (during the rule of his son, (Partha), was at last, crowned king after the removal of Partha from the throne.[217] But he was destined not to rule long and died in 923 A.D. After nominating Chakravarman, his child son, to the throne, Nirjitavarman had every opportunity both as a regent and finally as a ruler to have distinguished himself as a capable ruler; instead he proved a moral leper and was addicted to cups. He never cared for the welfare of the people and was content to look to his own pleasures and comforts.

Chakravarman was for some time under the guardianship of his mother, Bappatadevi, and then for ten years under that of his grandmother, Ksillika.[218] Then in 933-4 the Tantrins overthrew Cakravarman and made Suravarman-I, the son of Pangu from Mrgavati, king.[219]

Yasaskara ruled for nine years (A.D.939-948). He had been selected as king by an assembly of Brahmans called together for this specific purpose by the commander-in-chief who had driven out his predecessor. Yasakara proved to be a good and just ruler. In his time the land became free from robbery and the rapacity of the officials.[220] Ashe exercised careful supervision, the functionaries, who had plundered everything, found no other occupation but to look after the cultivation.

Yasaskara is also credited with foundation of several religious shrines, which included a monastery. The King was so social that he mixed freely even with low caste people like Dombas. In the later days of his life he is said to have fell seriously ill and he nominated Varnata, the son of his paternal grand uncle Ramadeva as his heir. But the latter incurred his displeasure by foolish acts as a result of which the crown finally fell upon Samgramadeva, a minor son of Yasaskara.[221]

Yasaskara's illegitimate son was killed by the wicked minister Parvagupta within a few months of his accession. Parvagupta, was son of samgramagupta, who had been born in parevisoka from a writer (divira) called Abhinava[222]. He obtained kingship after so much treachery, but he too was not destined to enjoy it for more than a year and a half. During his short reign he is said to have oppressed the people and exacted the money from them. To perpetuate his memory he founded with his ill-gotten wealth the shrine of Shiva, called Parvaguptesvara near the site of the Skandabhavanavihara.[223]

Parvagupta was succeeded by son Ksemagupta[224], a worthless young man addicted to licentious habits and drinking, and fond of evil company. In the hands of "Vamana and other roguish sons of Jisnu" he danced as if he were a doll pulled by strolling players with strings. During his reign Kashmir saw one of the worst periods of her history. His court was full of harlots, knaves, and depraved fellows. He earned lasting infamy by burning down the magnificent Jayendravihara erected in the time of Pravarasena. He got the noble edifice destroyed because of feudal lord had taken refuge in it to escape death at the hands of his assassins. Taking from this *Vihara*, which was entirely burned down, the brass of Sugata (Buddha), and collecting a mass of stones from decaying temples, he erected the temple of Shiva Ksemagaurisvara.[225]

Ksemagupta's reign is important in the history of Kashmir by reason of his marriage to Didda, daughter of Simharaja, the lord of Lohara, and grand-daughter of the Sahi ruler Bhima.[226] From this time onward the influence of the Sahi and the house of Lohara gradually increased in the Kashmirian court and had important consequences on its future history. Didda so much engrossed the mind of the king that he became known by the humiliating appellation Diddaksema.[227] After the death of her husband, Didda acted as a regent to her young son Abhimanyu[228]. There were a number of uprisings which she cleverly put down by bribing some and exterminating the other ringleaders. On her death secured the throne for her nephew, Samgramaraja, the sin of the ruler of Lohara.

Samgramaraja[229] was a weak ruler. He retained Tunga as his prime minister who is said to have enjoyed maximum powers. The prime minister cut off the maintenance allowances of the gods, cows, Brahmanas, the orphans and the guests and oppressed the people by various fiscal exactions, made him unpopular. The period of Samgramaraja on the other hand witnessed a great calamity in the shape of Mahmud Ghazni's invasion. The invader advanced to the very confines of Kashmir but was fortunately prevented from entering the valley by its high mountain walls and an early fall of snow.

At the last stage of king, there was some sort of rivalry between the king's favourites at the court and in administration on the other hand and the powerful Damras and Dards on the other hand. After ruled about 26 years he died in 1028 A.D. and was succeeded by his son Hariraja[230] who is said to have ruled only for 22 days. According to Kalhana, it was generally claimed that the ambitious and libidinous queen (Srilekha, his mother) was responsible for the death of Hariraja.[231] She killed her son by the use of witchcraft and tried to seize the throne as queen Didda. Against the ambitions of queen nobles of state under Ekanga, installed Ananta,[232] his younger brother to the throne.

The Shahi princes and noblemen enjoyed great influence in the time of Ananta, and were a source of great oppression to the people. One of the, Anangapala, who was a favourite of the king was ever planning the breaking of the golden statues of grids,[233] another Rudrapala, patronised murderers[234] and robbers. The Shahi noblemen drew high salaries and at one time Ananta was reduced to such straits that he had to pawn his diadem.

After the death of two Shahi princes, Ananta came under the influence of his pious queen, Suryamati.[235] She checked the extravagance and vagaries of the king, and gradually assumed full charge of royal affairs. She made of religious foundations and gifts. She founded mathas in the name of her two brothers and husband[236]. But soon Ananta on the advice of queen abdicated the throne in the favour of his son Kalasa.[237] When a severs famine broke out in the country in 1063 A.D.[238] Ananta however, retained some powers for himself till 1076, when he retired to the sacred town of Vijayesvara along with his stores and treasure. Kalasa burnt the town and insisted on sending his aged father to exile. Ananta, latter on committed suicide in 1081 A.D. His wife Suryamati ended her life as Sati.[239]

After the death of his father, Kalsa assumed full powers. He was also assisted by his son Harsha in his administration. Kalsa was an able ruler. He is said to have brought peace and prosperity to his kingdom by initiating improvement in his administration[240]. But he was also a profligate prince and had as many as seventy two women in his seraglio. Most of these had been procured by Muslim attendants of his who hailed from the Punjab. Kalasa confiscated the villages which formed the endowments of some temples.

The last years of Kalasa were embittered by the disunion and suspicion between himself and Harsha. Thus Harsha conspired against his father but was arrested in 1088 A.D[241]. Kalasa installed his other son Utkarsha to the throne. Harsha, who was in prison now hatched a conspiracy against Utkarsha with his step brother Vijayamalla and thus seized the throne. Young Utkarsha barely 24 year of age finally committed suicide in the prison after being on the throne for only 22 days; the right full claimant to the throne was thus finally rewarded with his due.[242] Before his death Kalasa had passes the crown Utkarsa but Harsha overturned him.

Harsha came to the throne in 1089[243]. He was remarkable person in many ways. Possessed of exceptional powers, he obtained renown by merits rarely to be found in other kings.

Versed in many languages, goo poet, a lover of music and arts, and a repository of different branches of learning, he became famous in other kingdoms also.[244] He adopted wise policy by retaining many of his father's officials and trusted servants. He led expeditions to several hilly principalities adjoining to valley. Samgrama Pala the lord of Rajuri was defeated and forced to pay tribute.[245] He is said to have introduced many new fashions in dress and ornaments.

But a curious transformation seems to have come over him later in his reign when he developed Nero- like propensities. His love of pomp and show and his extravagant expenditure on his troops and favourites led him into financial difficulties. Urgent necessity for money at last turned the liberal king into a cruel oppressor. Harsha not only annexed the treasures of the temple, but also appointed officers called devotpatananayaka to desecrate temples and then to overthrow the divine images which could be sold at their metal value. He was further reduced to the necessity of levying new and oppressive imports. Even night soil became the object of taxation.[246]

Uchchala, who elder son of Sassala now came to the throne, represented the beginning of the second Lahora dynasty.[247] He was on the whole energetic and capable ruler. After reigning ten years, he was however, himself murdered.

Jayasimaha, now became the king[248]. He proved to be a capable ruler who gave to his country much needed peace and good government. Jayasimha seems to have been a statesman of high calibre. He realized that his position could be maintained only if the turbulent Damras could be kept in check. The royal authority was not strong enough to suppress these feudal lords. So he adopted the strategy of playing one powerful Damra against another. Furthermore according to Kalhana that Jayasimha won the support of Damras by bribing them. *Bhikashchara* was compelled to retire from Kashmir and was finally killed in 1130 A.D. Finding that there was no pretender on the scene, whom they could use as a tool, the Damras were demoralized one by one.[249] Jayasimha thus stabilize his empire and after established peace in the land, he devoted his time in numerous building activities. During the last five years of his reign, he undertook a successful expedition against a Muslim ruler (*Yavana Turuska*), who however cannot be identified. The rule of Jayasimha ended in 1155 A.D. and was succeeded by his son Parmanudeva who ruled for ten years. With the assistance of two officers *Prayag* and *Janaka*, he filled up his royal treasury. Neither did he protect his subjects, nor did he undertake any expedition abroad. Parmanudeva was succeeded by his son Vanetadeva, who died in 1171 A.D,[250] after an uneventful seven years. With his death the second Lohara dynasty came to an end.

After the death of Jayasimha the country again reverted to its chronic state of decrepitude. The two centuries that elapsed between the passing away of Jayasimha and the transfer of the throne to the Muslim Shah Mir produced no king possessing genius enough to consolidate his kingdom.

In the time of Simhadeva (1286-1300 A.D) and his brother Sahadeva(1300-1320A.D) Kashmir was a country of drunkards, gamblers and profligate women. During the reign of Sahadeva Kashmir was invaded by Zulchu(Dulcha). Instead of facing him manfully, the king fled to Kishtwar. Dulcha plundered the people, took slaves and set fire to the city of Srinagar. Sahadea's commander in chief, Ram Chandra saved the valley from the invasion of Dulucha. Henceforth Sahandeva disappears. Then Ramachandra reigned over valley. Two men remaining with him were Richina and Shah Mir. Rinchina then killed Ramachandra and married Kota Rani and proclaimed himself king in 1320A.D. with Shah Mir who had been loyal to him.

After the death of Richina, the throne was occupied by Udayanadeva, he also married Kota Rani. At this time Kashmir was invaded by Achala a Mongol Turk. The king Udayanadeva, like his brother fled away from Kashmir. Shah Mir defended the kingdom successfully in his absence. When the invader, had been cleverly sent away, the king Udayanadeva returned but with no strength. He died in

1338A.D. and Kota Rani assumed power, but only for few months. Shah Mir deposed Kota Rani and proclaimed himself king. He was the first of the Sultans of Kashmir.

REFERENCES

1. R.T*, Vol-ii, p. 386.
   *Kalhana's *Rajatrangini*, translated by M.A. Stein
2. A.R. Khan, *Geography of Jammu and Kashmir*, Srinagar, 2007, p. 1
3. W.R. Lawrence, *The Valley of Kashmir*, p. 44.
4. *Ibid.*
   Lydekkar, *The Geology of Kashmir and Chamba*, p. 72.
5. M.A. Stein., *Ancient Geography*, p. 64.
6. *Ibid.*
   Frederick Drew., *The Jammu and Kashmir Territory*, p. 162.
7. H.C. Ray., *Dynastic History of Northern India*, Vol, I, P. 107.
8. M.A. Stein, *Ancient Geography.*, p. 70
9. *Ibid.* 88
10. Walter Lawrence, *The Valley of Kashmir*, p. 14.
11. *Ibid.* 31
12. Frederick Drew., *op.cit.*, p. 180.
13. S.L. Shali, *Kashmir History and Archaeology through the Ages*, New Delhi, 1993, p. 19.
14. R.T., Vol. II. pp. 351-355.
15. Mcrindle, *Ancient India by Ptolemy*, p. 108
16. H.H. Wilson, *The Hindu History of Kashmir*, p. 114.
17. R.T., Vol. II., p. 352.
18. R.T., Vol. II., 354.
19. R.T., Vol. II. p. 355.
20. *Ibid.*
21. *Ibid.*
22. Pelctch Luciano, *A Study on the Chronicles of Ladakh*, p. 12.
23. G.M.G. Sufi, *Kashir*, p. 12.
24. R.T., Vol. II., p. 357.
25. *Ibid* 358.
26. According to Buhler (1877) The *Nilamatapurana* was written in the 6th and 7th century A.D.
27. Ved Kumari, *Nilamata Purana*, pp. 16,17.
28. R.T., I, 25. 26. 27.

29. Ved kumari, *op.cit.*, 46.
30. Shafi Ahmad Qadri, op.cit, p. 2
31. Ved kumari, *op.cit.*, p. 46
32. S.L. Shali, *Kashmir History and Archaeology through the Ages*, p. 47.
33. R.T., I., 48-49.
34. R.T., I., 50-63.
35. R.T., I., 64.
36. R.T., I., 65-70.
37. R., T., I., 74. 75. 76.
38. R.T., I., 83.
39. R.T., I., 84-99.
40. S.C. Ray, *Early History and Culture of Kashmir*, Srinagar, 2008, p. 44.
41. S.L.S.Sodhi, The History of Ancient Kashmir, Srinagar, 2006, p. 16.
42. R.T., I., 101.
43. *Ibid.*
44. P.N.K. Bamzi., Cultural and political History of Kashmir., p. 217
45. R.T. I., 101, 102, 103.
46. R.T., I., 105. 106.
47. R.T., I., 104.
48. S.L. Shali, *op.cit.*, p.118
49. R.T., I., 108.
50. R.T., I., 115, 116, 117
51. R.T., I., 117.
52. R.T., I., 113.
53. G.M.D. Sufi., *op.cit.*, p. 40.
54. R.T., I., 136.
55. R.T., I., 131-146.
56. R.T., I., 153.
57. R.T., I., 157.
58. R.T., I., 156-166.
59. R.T., I., 168.
60. *ibid*
61. S.L.Shali, *op.cit.*, p. 123.
62. J.N. Ganhar, P.N. Ganhar, Buddhism in Kashmir and Ladakh , pp. 29-30.
63. Shafi Ahmad Qadri, op.cit., p. 5.
64. S.L. Shali, *op.cit.*, p. 123.

65. R.T., I., 174.
66. R.T., I., 175.
67. R.T., I., 176.
68. R.T., I., 177.
69. R.T., I., 174-184.
70. R.T., I., 182.
71. R.T., I., 189.
72. H.H. Wilson, *op.cit.*, pp.23-24.
73. *Ibid.*
74. R.T., I., 197.
75. J.C. Dutt., Kings of Kashmir, Vol. II, p. 15.
76. R.T., I., 199-200.
77. R.T., I., 201-202
78. R.T., I., 276.
79. R.T., I., 286.
80. R.T., I., 287.
81. R.T., I., 288.
82. R.T., I., 289.
83. R.T., I., 291.
84. R.T., I., 306-307.
85. R.T., I., 312-316.
86. R.T., I., 289-324.
87. R.T., I., 325.
88. R.T.,I., 329.
89. R.T., I., 330.
90. R.T., I.,., 337.
91. R.T., I., 338.
92. R.T., I., 340.
93. R.T., I., 341.
94. R.T., I., 334.
95. R.T., I., 346.
96. R.T.,I., 347.
97. R.T., I., 347.
98. R.T., I., 349.
99. R.T., I., 350.
100. R.T., I., 350-373.
101. R.T., II., 5

102. R.T., II., 7.
103. R.T., II., 9.
104. R.T., II., 11.
105. R.T., II., 14.
106. R.T., II., 16.
107. R.T., II., 62.
108. R.T., II., 63, 64, 65.
109. R.T., ii., 65.
110. R.T., II., 65-171.
111. R.T., III., 5. 6. 7.
112. R., T., III., 27.
113. R.T., III., 8.
114. R.T., III., 9.
115. R.T., III., 10.
116. R.T., III., 11.
117. R.T., III., 13.
118. R.T., III., 97.
119. R.T., III., 99.
120. R.T., III., 102.
121. R.T., III., 103 104.
122. R.S. Pandit, *op.cit.*, pp. 94-101.
123. *ibid.*
124. *ibid*
125. *Ibid.* p. 102
126. M.L. Kapour, *op.cit.*, p. 26.
127. R.T., IV., 2.
128. S.L. Shali, *op.cit.*, p-148.
129. R.T., III., 490.
130. R.T., ii., p. 355.
131. R.T., IV., 7.
132. R.T., IV., 32.
133. R.T., IV., 11-43.
134. R.T., IV., 45.
135. *ibid.*
136. *K.S. Saxena, op.cit.*, p. 47.
137. R.T., IV., 119.
138. R.T., IV., 126.

139. R.T., IV., 131.
140. R.T., IV., 136-144.
141. R.T., IV., 148-171.
142. W. Lawarence, *The Valley of Kashmir*, p 186.
143. K.S. Saxena., *op.cit.*, p 50-52.
144. R.T., IV., 194.
145. J.C. Chatterji, A note on the Confluence of the *Vitasta* and the Sindh in Kashmir- Appendix D published with a brief statement of works done by the Archaeology and research Department J & K State, Srinagar, p. 39.
146. R.T., IV., 295-199.
147. R.T., IV., 192.
148. P.N.K Bamzi, op. cit., p. 143.
149. G.M.D. Sufi., *op.cit*, p. 53.
150. R.T., IV., 188.
151. R.T., IV., 210.
152. R.T., IV., 211, 215, 216, 262.
153. R.T., IV., 372.
154. R.T., IV., 372 -392.
155. R.T., IV., 393.
156. R.T., IV., 395. 396.
157. *Ibid.*
158. R.T., IV, 398.
159. R.T., IV., 399.
160. RR. T., IV., 400.
161. R.T., IV., 402.
162. R.T., IV., 414.
163. R.T., IV., 421.
164. R.T., IV., 468-471.
165. R.I., IV., 570.
166. R.T., IV., 506.
167. R.T., IV., 512.
168. R.T., V., 2.
169. *Ibid.*
170. P.N.K. Bamzi *op.cit.*, 150.
171. *Ibid.*
172. M.L. Kapur, *Studies in History and Culture of Kashmir*, Jammu, 1976, p. 17.

173. R.T., Vol-I. p. 97.
174. R.T., V., 44.
175. G.M.Rabbani, Kashmir Social and Cultural History, Srinagar, 2007, p. 27.
176. R.T., V., 45.
177. R.T., V., 46.
178. R.T., V., 32-36.
179. R.T., V., 68
180. R.T., V., 69, 70, 71.
181. R.T., V., 72-79.
182. Somanath Dhar, Tales of Kashmir, New Delhi, 1992, pp. 24-25.
183. R. T., V., 79-117.
184. R.T., V., 119.
185. R.T., V., 39.
186. R.T., V., 120.
187. R.T., V., 121.
188. R.T., V., 123.
189. R.T., V., 126, 127, 128.
190. Somnath Dhar, *op. cit.*, p. 84.
191. P.N.K. Bamzai, *op. cit.*, p. 138.
192. M.A. Stein, *op. cit.*, p. 99.
193. *Ibid.*
194. *Ibid.*
195. R.T., V., 156.
196. R.T., V., 161.
197. Percy Brown, *Indian Architecture (Buddhist and Hindu)*, Bombay, 1959, p. 48.
198. R.C.Kak, *Ancient Monuments of Kashmir*, New Delhi, 1971, p. 120.
199. R.T., V., 166.
200. R.T., V., 167
201. R.T., V., 168.
202. R.T., V., 174.
203. R.T., V., 228.
204. R.T., V., 230, 231.
205. R.T., V., 232, 233.
206. R.T., V., 242.
207. R. T., V., 243.

208. R.T., V., 244.
209. H.H.Wilson, *The Hindu History of Kashmir*, Srinagar, 2006, pp. 64-65.
210. *Ibid*.
211. R.T., V., 253-255.
212. R.T., V., 264.
213. R.T., V., 266.
214. R.T., V., 271.
215. R.T., V., 272, 273.
216. R.T., V., 274.
217. R.T., V., 287.
218. R.T., V., 290.
219. R.T., V., 292.
220. R.T., VI., 2-7.
221. R.T., VI., 2-114.
222. R.T., VI., 128-130.
223. R.T., VI., 137.
224. R.T., VI., 150.
225. R.T., VI., 171-173.
226. R.T., VI., 167.
227. R.T., VI., 177.
228. R.T., VI., 188-292.
229. R.T., VII., 2-126.
230. R.T., VII., 127.
231. R.T., VII., 134-135.
232. *Ibid*.
233. R.T., VII., 147.
234. R.T., VII., 149.
235. R.T., 179.
236. R.T, VII., 180-185.
237. R.T., VII., 230-231.
238. *Ibid*.
239. R.T., VII 317-452.
240. R.T., VII., 424-590.
241. R.T., 627-680.
242. R.T., VII., 723-829.
243. R.T., VII., 829.
244. P.N.K Bamzi., *op. cit*., p. 175.

245. R.T., VII., 967-980.
246. R.T., VII., 1100-1107.
247. R.T., VIII., 2.
248. R.T., VIII., 1350-1355.
249. P.N.K. Bamzai, *op. cit.*, p. 187.
250. J.C. Dutt, *Kings of Kashmir, an English Trans. of Jonaraja's Rajtarangini*, Delhi, 1986, p. 49.

2

Social Organisation

It is indeed unfortunate that very little information is available on the social and economic conditions in ancient Kashmir. Early works like *Nilmatapurana*, the *Kuttanimata Kavya* and the writings of Ksemendra make here and there only passing references on the subject. We have, therefore, to fall back mainly on Kalhana's *Rajatarangini*.

Castes of People

A close study of Kalhana's work shows that society in ancient Kashmir comprised several castes, such as Brahmans, Nisadas, Kiratas, Dombas, Chandalas and Svapakas. But the adamantine rigidity, which marked the caste system in India, was absent in Kashmir. This was, perhaps, due to the influence of Buddhism which flourished here quite early.[1] Under king Chakravarman, for instance, the Dombas practically filled all the prestigious posts in the court. Two of his queens also belonged to this caste.[2] No wonder, we find in the history of this country many men and women belonging to low castes occupying positions of trust and responsibility.[3]

Another point which strikes reader's mind so forcibly is the absence of such castes as Kashatriyas, Vaisas and Sudras, although the conception of the population as consisting of the four traditional castes was not altogether unknown in early Kashmir.[4]

The Brahmanas, variously referred to Vipra, Dvija, Dvijanman and Agrajanman, undoubtly occupied the more privileged and the more honoured position in the society.[5] They were considered very pious and their curse could misery (*dukkha*)[6]. It was a religious duty to respect them. The occupations pursued by them were varied. A vast majority of them was, however, engaged in the study of scriptures and the calling of priests and teachers.[7] Some of them joined government service and worked not only in civil but also military departments. Many Brahmanas are known to have been appointed to high officials. Kalhana refers to a Brahmana named Rakka, who was very popular on account of his bravery[8]. Damodaragupta himself, as we learn from Kalhana, was the chief minister of king Jayapida.[9] Thus we see that *Mitrasarman*, the chief minister of Lalitaditya, *Devasarman*, a minister of Jayapida, and *Phalguna*, the chief minister of Didda, were all Brahmans, so were Bujanga, Campaka and Ajjaka, Lovaraja and Yasoraja in the times of Samgramaraja, Harsa and Sussala respectively, who held military posts and took active part in fighting.[10] Ajjaka, a Brahman minister of Salhana died in the battlefield while fighting against Sussala[11]. Kalyanaraja, was a Brahman solider well versed in military exercises[12]. Kalhanas father Canpaka was the dvarapati of Harsha[13]. Thus it may be said that the rules and regulations prescribed by our ancient lawgivers were not strictly followed, and the Brahmanas adopted professions of other castes according to their choice and convenience. Kalhana refers, that Brahmana Sivarath was appointed as Kayastha official[14]. As we know that it was duty of king to protect the *Varnasrama* in ancient India the king who was religious, strict, tried to regulate the cast system. An interesting illustration of this strictness was narrated by Kalhana. He stated that 'king Yasaskar was ever ready to exercise control over the castes and conditions of life among his subjects. On discovery that at Chakramela, a Brahman ascetic named Chakabhanu had departed from proper conduct, in accordance with Dharma, the king punished him, by 'branding his forehead the mark of dog *foot*[15].

The Brahmanas were given lesser punishment in comparison to the members of other castes. Alberuni states that if a Brahman killed a man, he had only to fast, pray, and give alms[16]. We see that the rulers and aristocrats of the period gave recognition to the intellectual superiority of the Brahmanas by giving various grants and gifts to them[17]. Kalhana states that the Brahmanas still possessed the power of selecting a king or rejecting a nominated king. In Kashmir Brahmanas nominated king Yasaskar in preference to Kamal Vardhan[18]. Besides sacrificial fees, the main source of their income was the revenue derived from the land-grants or *Agraharas* donated by the Kings and other rich people.[19] It follows from this that the Brahmans in Kashmir were mainly dependent on land and, therefore, formed a class of small landlords. Donations were also frequently made to them.[20] The *Nilamatapurana* indeed considers it a meritorious act if someone gave them gifts on the occasion of a religious ceremony. The temple priests also pocketed the revenue of the villages endowed to the temples. It is interesting to note that they made a further pile not only by selling flowers, incense, etc. To the devotees but also by reselling the latter's offerings to the public. The life of the Brahmans was thus such that it involved little expenditure of energy.

Kalhana records that Brahmanas from Sindh and even persons from the far off Dravida land settled in Kashmir during the reign of king Jayasimha[21]. Probably, there had been several large scale immigrations of the Brahmanas from the plains of India into the valley of Kashmir from a remote period[22]. The descendants of these immigrants seem to have composed the bulk of the Brahmana population of Kashmir.

Rajaputras or Rajputs, the traditional fighting caste in Indian society, are also referred to by Kalhana in his work. Although these references are few, Tantrins[23], Ekangas[24] and Laveny[25] as are, however, much spoken of, all of them seem to have been the tribes of professional soldiers who formed, at later times, into formidable groups and virtually acted as king-makers.[26]

Nisadas[27] were probably the aboriginal tribes and occupied a very low position in the social ladder. They earned their livelihood by following such calling as hunting, boating and fishing.

Kiratas lived in the forests and made their both ends meet by killing wild animals. Both professions, therefore, they were close to Nisadas and both were looked down upon.

The Dombas[28] were a caste of menials. Their professions included hunting, singing and dancing. Sometimes Kalhana also calls them *Svapakas,* a term which literally means dog-cookers. The people invariably turned up their noses at them.

Another despised, low caste in ancient Kashmir was that of the Candalas[29]. Some of them were engaged as royal body-guards and watchmen. They also quite often came handy to wicked persons as assassins.

Classes of People

From the socio-economic standpoint, ancient people of Kashmir could be grouped into various classes according to the professions adopted by them. Like other contemporary society the Ancient Kashmir society was a class ridden society i.e., there were different sections of the society with different economic condition. The basic cause of the economic differentiation of the society was that the source or the means of production namely land and capital were owned and controlled by a few individuals. The upper class consisted of the ruling family and ministers who got large share out of production and lived a luxurious life. There was private ownership of wealth. State interference in private enterprises was very little.[30]

Among all these groups Damras certainly was the powerful one. Damras played a vital role in early Kashmir. But the origin of the name Damras is shrouded in mystery. According to M.L.Kapur, "the exact meaning of the term Damra is, however, still a guess work, it is frequently referred to by Kshemendra, Kalhana, Jonaraja and Srivara, but none of them has tried to give its meaning."[31] According to H.H.Wilson, "Damras were fierce tribe, inhabiting the mountains to the north of Kashmir."[32]

The difficulties which it involved had not escaped authors of the St. Petersburg Dictionary who, with reference to a possible etymology, suggested that the word might have had originally a more general meaning, 'riotous rebel'. But the true purport of the term was recognised only in a brief supplementary note that work which reproduces a suggestion of professor H. Kern assigning to Damra the meaning 'Bojar,' i.e. feudal land owner or baron.[33]

Kalhana's first reference to the Damras appears in the fourth Taranga, were among the maxims set forth by Lalitaditya is one directing the rulers to prevent hoarding of wealth by powerful landlords as otherwise they would be powerful and rich Damras and defy orders of the king[34]. According to M.L.Kapur, "this passage leaves us with no doubt the fact that the agriculturists were transformed into powerful Damras when they acquired considerable wealth."[35] With the passage of time they became powerful and interfering in the political affairs of state. During the reign of Avantivarman one of these Damras, Dhanva, a powerful Damara of the district (Lahore) is said to have usurped the villages endowed to the temple Bhutesvara. Dhanva, who owes his unrestrained local predominance to the patronage of the king's powerful minister Sura, neglects summons after summons. At last, when he appeared before the minister, he made the earth shake with the tramp of his host of foot soldiers and did not bend his back.[36]

About the middle of the 10th centutyA.D., the Damras became so powerful that they began to interfere in the questions of royal succession. When king Cakravarman had been driven a second time from his capital bu his mutinous praetorians, the Tantrins, he took refuge with Samgrama, an influential Damra, resident in Madavarajya. After the conclusion of a solemn compact the Damras rose in support of the deposed king, and with the help of others of his class, who joined him, succeeded in reinstating him. But after words, when Cakravarman alienated the Damras, he was ultimately murdered by these turbulent feudal chiefs.[37]

There is comparatively little mention made of Damaras in the later part of fifth book and in the next. But there are characteristic indications of their growing influence even during the period of comparative consolidation which followed Yasakara's accession and queen Didda's advent to power. Didda was the first who tried to control them. With the accession of Lohara house, the Damras appear in their fullest power. They virtually became the king makers after Didda's death. During the long succession of weak reigns from Samgramaraja to Utkarsa's death, the position of the Damaras as semi-independent feudal lords seems firmly to have established itself. In the struggle for the throne between Ananta and his son Kalasa, and between Utkarsha and Harsha, the Damras took the side of one or the other and final issue of the conflict depended mostly on their support.[38] By the end of 12th century, the Damras had become powerful. They had enormous wealth, a large army and strong holds in many important places of the valley.[39] They placed Ucchala and Sussala on the throne of Kashmir and earned their favour. Ucchala remained in dander because of high handedness of Damaras who had helped him in securing the throne. One of the Damara chieftains, Gargacandra became a king maker in the true sense of the term. In the conflict between the pretender Bhiksacara on the one hand and Sussala and Jayasimha on the other, that party alone could expect a victory which powerful Damaras at its back. They were so powerful and influential that, "even royal families entering into matrimonial alliances with them."[40] Their fortified residences were called *Upavesana*, which were like the castles of medieval feudal lords.[41] They had hereditary rights over their lands. They even engaged themselves in trade and commerce and acquire wealth. It is important to mention here that Damras did not belong to any particular caste or tribe but where from different groups of society.[42]

Second most important class was of Kayasthas who remained in the service of kings. "The term Kayastha did not denote any particular caste, but applied to all the members of bureaucracy-from the lowest clerk to the highest official. The Kayastha include such specific officers as *grhakrtyyadhipati* or *grhakrtyamahattama* or simple *mahatama, paripalaka, margesa* or *margapati, ganjadhipa, nagaradhipa, saulkika, niyogi, adhikaranalekhaka, asvaghasakayastha, gramakayastha* and *diviras* of *nagara, ganja* etc.,[43] The term Kayastha was applied to the officials in the king's service. Kalhana refers them as officials.[44] M.L.Kapur however subdivided them into two classes-the nobility and bureaucracy. Kalhana says that Kayastha career was open to all. Even persons holding other hereditary occupations, sometimes lowly ones that of *aramika* (gardener) could enter into the rank of Kayastha.[45] But it seems that Brahman dominating this profession.[46]

The epigraphic records and the literature of the period reveal that the Kayastha became very powerful, and rose to the highest public officers in different fields. As they became an important class of the society they attracted the attention of the society and perhaps out of curiosity people began to comment and tell stories about the lineage of the Kayasthas.

The Kayasthas drew their salaries from the royal treasury probably every month. Besides being a salary class, they were notorious for illegal exactions, corruption and bribery which were mentioned in their works by Kshemendra and Kalhana. But due to their efficiency in conducting the day to day administration, the Kayasthas, particularly during the later centuries of Hindu rule, acquired enormous power. It was for their capacity to raise new taxes, that the kings of Kashmir became habituated to looking at faces of the Kayasthas for quittance, and to following the direction of their servants.[47] In fact, all sorts of officials from the highest administrative to the lowest clerical, whose principal duty, besides carrying on the general administration on the state consisted in the collection of revenue and taxes.[48] Ksemendra has stated that Kayasthas were in charge of collecting revenue govern a province, supervise confidential records and accounts, and control the treasury etc.[49] It was because of their talent that kings like to take their services. Some kings like Ucchala tried to curb their power but their success proved to be only temporary.[50] But because of their notorious activities, according to Bamzai, they had to leave the valley. Their vacancies were filled by Kashmiri *Pandiths* who were well read.[51]

From the available sources it may be presumed that the 10th century A.D., the Kayasthas formed a caste, and by the last quarter of 11th century A.D., The caste had several sub-groups. Literary and epigraphic records give numerous examples of Kayasthas as scribers. Sometimes they took other professions.[52] Thus we see Kayasthas became a caste during the period under review. They also played an important role in the society.

The lower class comprised of the peasants, artisans and craftsmen. Notwithstanding the fact that they were the backbone of the society, majority of people belong to this group, they were primary producers. But their condition was not good. Some of them were tenants of Damras,[53] and sometimes work as agricultural labours for wages. Some had their own land that had to fulfil high land revenue demand of state. They were further squeezed by the Kayasthas.

In short, the production relations who were essentially feudalistic in character accounted for a class ridden society, where a small section enjoyed a luxurious life and masses suffered for barest needs.

REFERENCES

1. P.N.KBamzai, *Culture and Political History if Kashmir*, Vol. I, Delhi, 1994. p. 211.
2. M.L.Kapur, *Studies in History and Culture of Kashmir*, Jammu, 1976, p. 66.
3. P.N.K.Bamzai, *op. cit.*, p. 212.
4. S.C.Ray, *Early History and Culture of Kashmir*, Srinagar, 2008, p. 112.
5. M.L.Kapur, *op. cit.*, p. 67.
6. Sarla Khosla, *op.cit.*,133.

7. *Ibid.*
8. R.T.V. 424.
9. R.T, IV. 496.
10. *Ibid.*
11. R.T., VIII, 472.
12. R.T., VII., 1071.
13. R.T., VIII., 1177.
14. RT., VIII, 2383.
15. R.T., VI, 108, 109.
16. E.C. Sochau, *Alburunis india.*, I, P. 101.
17. R.T., II., 55., III., 376, 481.
18. R.T., V, 469-77.
19. M.L.Kapur, *op. cit.*, p. 67.
20. P.N.K. Bamzai, *op. cit.*, p. 213.
21. R.T. VIII., 2444
22. The earliest inscriptional reference of the Brahmanas occurs in the edict of Asoka, where they have been mentioned as one of the most important classes among the population of the Maurya empire. Since the valley of Kashmir was included within Asokas empire, it is not quite unlikely that the Brahmanas from other parts of india had come to live in Kashmir by the time of Asoka.
23. R.T., V 248.
24. R.T., V 249, 250
25. R.T VII. 1171
26. *Ibid.*
27. As designation for boatmen, R.T., V., 101
28. A low caste of menials, R. T., IV 475
29. Used as watchmen. R. T., IV 475
30. S.C.Ray, *op. cit.*, p. 119.
31. M.L.Kapur, *op. cit.*, p. 68.
32. H.H.Wilson, *The Hindu History of Kashmir*, Srinagar, 2000, p. 151.
33. R.T., Vol. II, p. 304.
34. R.T., IV., 348.
35. M.L. Kapur, *op. cit.*, p. 68.
36. R.T., V., 51-60.
37. R.T., V., 306-308, 326-328, 405-410.
38. R.T., VII., 154, 167, 357, 765, 914.

39. R.T., VII., 1254., viii., 648, 929, 1124, 1153, 2505.
40. *Ibid.*
41. *Ibid.*
42. *Ibid.*
43. S.C. Ray, *Early history and culture of Kashmir*, p. 111.
44. R.T., IV., 90-92, 621-29.
45. R.T., VII., 39-41
46. R.T., VIII, 2383.
47. R.T., VI., 623.
48. S.C. Ray, *op. cit.*, pp. 103-04.
49. R.T., IV., 90.
50. J.C.Dutt, *Kings of Kashmir* (tran's. of Kalhan's, Jonaraja and Srivara's Rajtarangini-3 Vols.), Calcutta, 1887, p. 8.
51. P.N.K. Bamzai, *op. cit.*, p. 235.
52. R.T., IV., 90-92, 621-29.
53. R.T., Vol. II. p. 495.

3

Marriage and Position of Women

Awareness of women's role in social reconstruction and progress has now become almost universal. The great service rendered by women in the various vocations of life as mothers, wives, sisters, daughters, teachers, friends etc has contributed substantially to the march of civilization everywhere in human society. Consequently, in every social organization, women have been considered as important as men, though the fact is clearly recognized only in highly cultured societies and forms, in the opinion of many, the best means of judging the standard that a society has reached in its culture[1].

The active role that women all over the world have played in all spheres of life including liberation movements has betrayed their inherent strength and potentialities. Social reforms and political leaders have realized that without the progress of its women folk, the progress of a country is not possible. A French man has ones observed that the best way to judge the position of a nation was to find out the position and status of its women. In the same strain, A.S. Altaker, the great historian in the opening sentences of his noted work, The " *position of women in Hindu civilization*" observed, 'one of the best ways to understand the spirit of a civilization and to appreciate its excellence and realize its limitations, is to study the history of the position and status of women in it[2]. In Kashmir, however, the status of a woman was much better than in the rest of India. Here they were afforded opportunity to distinguish themselves in any sphere of social activity. As a matter of fact "They had emerged from the domestic into the political stage, were free, owned landed and other immovable property, managed their own estates and even fought on the battle field as generals and commanders at the head of troops several women have played a significant role in shaping the political history of Kashmir. We know that Sugandha[3], Didda[4], Srilekha[5], Suryamati[6], Anangalekha[7], Jayamati[8] and Kalhanika[9] played an important role not only in politics but in the field of administration also. Some of these queens were also engaged in the works of social welfare. In this region Nona proved to be a good diplomat. Silla and Chudda have shown their valour in military command. They proved their usefulness for their kingdoms at the time of crises. Suryamati the queen of king Ananta helped her husband to overcome his initial difficulties in administering the state. Queen Kalhanika, was sent on a delicate diplomatic mission of bringing about a rapprochement between Jayasimha and Bhoja.

One of the most note worthy features of early Kashmir society was that women had access to good and liberal education. The contemporary literature gives a vivid description of happy life of maidens or unmarried girls.[10] Our knowledge about women's education in Kashmir is meagre. Bilhana who was the poet Laureate at the court of Kalyan in Deccan (11th Century), gives in the last Canto of his book, a brief account of his motherland and its people, while describing the women of Kashmir, their beauty and accomplishments, the poet tills us that they spoke Sanskrit fluently.[11] Kalhana and other writers too have succinctly alluded to their scholarship and erudition. We have ample evidence to indicate that women during our period received a good deal of literary education and training in the practical and fine arts. [12]Abhinavagupta the brilliant theorist of the *Trika* has stressed that women have equal right with men to study philosophy and are as much eligible to take part in religious rites and rituals.[13] The curriculum of studies in the

9th century A.D. including the sexual science of Vatsyayana, Dattaka, Vitaputra and Rajaputra, the *Natyasastra* of Bharata, Visakhila's treatise on art, Dantila's work on music, *Urksayurveda*, painting, needlework, woodwork, metal work, clay modelling, cookery and practical training in instrumental music, singing and dancing.[14]

There is no reference to any veil worn by her and she moves quite freely in the society, emulating as it were the free-going sparking waters of the springs of her country.[15] The *Nilamata* allows her to participate in almost all the festivals and religious ceremonies. In the moonlit of Kaumudi Mahotsava, we find her setting beside the sacred fire in the company of her husband, children, servants and husband's friends. Not only on the festivals celebrated at home but also in the outdoor festivals, she is seen freely enjoying herself. Thus on the ceremonial day of ploughing the fields and sowing the seed, characterized by music, dancing and feasting, the peasant's wife is not behind the walls of her home. She is lucky enough to participate in the joyous festival celebrated in the refreshing open field of nature.[16]

Among common people, particularly the working class, both in villages and cities the veil was certainly unknown as in other parts of the country. The accounts of Ksemendra and Damodaragupta make it abundantly clear that working women did not use veil. Pen sketches of village women in *Kuttanimatam* which depict women going out of their homes for agricultural pursuits, for social congregations, for performing house jobs such as fetching water from wells, or bringing grass or wood from jungle and for joining religious processions.[17]

Women were allowed considerable freedom of movement. Even ladies of aristocratic families, who normally preferred to remain away from public gaze, came out of their houses on festive occasions and participate in the festivities freely as did other women who were not confined to their houses. They played dice with other women and, when engrossed in the festivities, did not shirk from using obscene words in public.[18]

Bamzai writes that there is no indication of women being kept in seclusion in Kashmir. The use of veil did not exist.

Regarding the proper age of marriage of a woman no positive evidence is forthcoming.[19] Marriages were arranged by the parents, but they did not play any role in the matters of remarriage.[20] A perusal of the *Rajatrangini* generally leaves the impression that pre-puberty marriage probably was not in vogue in ancient Kashmir.[21] It can safely be assumed from the circumstantial evidence of Damodragupta, Ksemendra, Kalahana and Jonaraja that she was not married before attaining 13-14 years of age.[22] The marriages were contracted between girls and boys of equal age or between a grown-up girl and an older male.[23] Sometimes a wealthy male of advanced age married a girl much younger than him in age. Obviously, such marriages between the partners of unequal age were not happy ones and the other brought public disapproval. Ksemendra narrates in his characteristic satirical way the wretched married life of an old man. The youthful wives in such marriages had to live a life of shame and frustration. They used to quarrel with their husbands and taunt them.[24] Marriage was to be performed at a mature age i.e. after the attainment of puberty and marriage was considered a religious necessity for both, men and women and a pre-requisite for the attainment of heaven.

Social organization in Kashmir was less rigid in comparison to that of many regions of south and middle India, and therefore various groups of people and communities had ample opportunities to mould themselves according to their choice. Geo-climatic conditions, contacts with foreigners and the deep impact of Buddhism had shattered the social fabric of Kashmir. Cast system in Kashmir was not rigid. May be, because of this, we find frequent cases of inter-caste marriages of Damara girls Gunalekha with jayasimha and Rajalaksmi with Sassala referred to earlier, of Narendara- prabha, a vaisya married lady with pratapaditya II of Hamsi and Nagalata, two domba girls with Cakravarman of, of kayya, a devedasi with kalasa, of sehaja, another devedasi with utkarasa are a few examples of inter-caste marriages. Sangramaraja, a ksatriya had given the hand of his sister to a Brahman. Similarly, vasanta, again a ksatriya had married his daughter to Damarakosthaka. There are numerous such examples of inter-caste marriages in ancient Kashmir[25].

Hindu law had already made provision of polygamy. It is therefore no surprise if we notice men having more than one living life. Polygamy was allowed in Kashmir and carried the stamp of social approval usually the ruling princes and the men of the upper classes had plurality of wives.[26] The poor or ordinary man took a second or third wife while one or more wives living only in special circumstances. Naturally polygamy created problems for co-wives and also for husband. Damodragupta presents a graphic picture of a man having many wives.[27] The poet describes the pitiable condition of a polygamous man [*bahujani*], one of whose wives is angered at her violation, another is indifferent because of the non fulfilment of her demand, another is sad as she has been denied a seat closely, forth maintains the distance because of mutual quarrel, and fifth, who is newly wedded, is too shy to behave with him freely[28]. Polyandry was quite unknown except perhaps among some aboriginal hill-tribes.[29] At one place Kalhana says, "The women which Kalhana enjoyed today, Losthana enjoyed the next day." We think this practice speaks of moral degradation and not of the existence of polyandry.[30] There were practically no restrictions on the liberty of man in this behalf. Often, most of these unfortunate ladies survived the death of their husbands. They were not allowed to have another partner in life as remarriage of windows was forbidden.[31]

Damodaragupta gives a graphic picture of an ideal wife; a wife borne of a noble family is the abode of all worldly pleasures; she follow her husband like reflection; she feels grieved in her husband's grief; she is happy when her husband is happy when her husband is worried, she is also worried; but when he gets enraged she is only timed she never speaks ill against him and always follows his mind; she also gave him full sexual pleasure those are fortunate indeed who have such a wife.

The lot of a housewife, particularly in rural areas, was an unenviable one. Hers was a wife of toil and hard work with little comfort. Damodaragupta gives us a beautiful word-picture of her life when she was tired after the hard work of the day and her body wet with sweat in the evening she went to a nearby well to fetch water she helped her husband in agricultural operations such as harvesting also she went to dense fields at some distance to pick up cotton fruits she unhooked paddy with the help of a pestles[32].

While the joint family system in India has been a boon to the society and a sort of society security for the members of the family, it has had some drawbacks too. It is difficult to say as to how young ladies reacted to the atmosphere of joint family when they came to their in-laws" house after their marriage, but some of them had some to live under strict – and sometimes harsh- control of their mothers in law. Even in the royal families, were the life was comfortable, easy and different from that of the common people, we find strict control over daughters –in – law. It was sometimes difficult for both mother-in-law and daughter-in-law to live together with peace and affection[33].

Widows were expected to live a pure life, devoid of all luxury. The ornaments or gorgeous dress forbidden to them, but the remarriage of widows and of other women does not seem to have been absolutely forbidden. We have the example of king Pratapaditya II marrying the wife of a rich merchant Nona. Kota Rain's remarriage with Udyanadeva after the death of her husband Rinchin, shows that widow marriage was permitted[34].

In almost all religious traditions marriage is one of the most sacred institutions. A women's devotion to her husband is seen as essential and very important to the marriage itself. They are expected to have this devotion not only when they are alive, but even after death. This could be proved through a ritual called *sati* where a widow was to be burnt alive on the funeral pyre of her husband so that she would be able to follow him even after his death.[35] The custom of burning of *sati* was in vogue in Kashmir from an early time.[36] Amongst various states of India except Bengal, Kashmir perhaps provides the maximum number of *sati* cases in her history. Here we find cases, where not only wives but even relatives of a deceased person immolated themselves.[37] In the stories of the *Kathasaritsagara,* which was composed in the valley in 11th C. A.D.? The custom appears to be quite common.[38] Damodaragupta calls the custom of *sati* as "duty of woman" (*Stridharma*).[39] The wide-spread currency of this custom is indicated by the numerous examples of courtesans who are said to have followed their lovers on funerary pyre[40]. Kalhana also has recorded several instances of queens, ladies of aristocratic families and even courtesans immolating themselves along with the dead bodies of their husbands and lover's[41]. The system of *sati* was not confined to the royal family alone. Malla, the wife of Bhogaseva, the chief-justice of Uccala followed her husband to death. Kalhana testified that the wife of Damara Kosthaka entered fire at the news of her husband's imprisonment and thus became a *sati*. Sometimes courtesans accompanied their masters into fire.[42] Jayamati a harlot of king Kalosa and Sahaja a concubine of king Utkarsa, entered the pyre of their masters. Damodaragupta relates about prostitutes performing the *sati* and immolating themselves. The custom of *sati* was so deep-rooted in the valley, that even mothers and sisters and other near relatives burnt themselves along with their beloved deceased. Gajja cremated herself with her son Ananda, Vallabha with her brother in law Malla and the sister of Dilhabhattaraka with her brother.[43] *Rajatrangini*is repeated with the instances of *sati*. When the dead body of the husband was available his wife burnt herself along with it but when it was not, she ascended a separate pyre even some days after his death as did for instance.[44]

Was committing of sati compulsory for a widow? Certainly not, we should not assume that it was obligatory for the widow to end her life after the death of her husband. The fact is that committing sati was optional and no compulsory was attached to it. There are many examples in the history of Kashmir wherein widows preferred to rule the country and enjoy political power and social recognition rather *anumarana* after the death of their husbands. It is worthy of note that not all wives of deceased king committed sati. All the queens of king Harsha did not commit sati. Didda, the famous ruler of Kashmir and Kotarani also did not commit sati[45].

But, despite the heinous custom of sati and ban on remarriage of widows, a Hindu woman had the right to freely choose her own partner in life. The institution of Swayamvara was as well known in Kashmir as in the rest of India. How far it obtained in the lower classes is controversial, but among the higher castes and wealthy sections, especially the Rajputs, it was a common practice. Love marriages are frequently mentioned in the annals and other literary works. A woman also enjoyed the right of separation and if dissatisfied with the marriage on rational grounds she could through mutual agreement with her husband, obtain a decree of divorce. Such a course was neither disapproved nor looked down upon even kings are known to have married divorced women nor the progeny of such marriages have subsequently ruled the land as monarchs in their hereditary right.[46]

The study of proprietary rights of women is a very fascinating subject. It has a vital importance for understanding the position of women in a particular period. It has been seen that proprietary rights of women were hardly recognised in any early civilization in a well methodical manner. They themselves were the items of movable property of the pariah. But it was not so in India.[47] On the question of inheritance and the division of property *Mitaksara and Dayabhaga* occupy very high places in Hindu law. *Dayabhaga* had its base and recognition especially in Bengal, but *Mitaksara* has been widely acceptable throughout India. According to *Mitaksara*, the widows and the daughters of a deceased person who had no son have the right of only maintenance. Further, if the successors of the deceased person do not divide the latter's property the women of the family can claim only their maintenance. While commenting on the prescriptions of Yajnavalkya on this matter, the Smrti Candrika opines that married daughters can get a part of the property of their father. It the latter divides his property, but in that event, they will surrender their share to their husbands. In certain commentaries of *Mitaksara* even a step mother is entitled for a portion of the property like mother since the son was assigned certain religious and sacramental obligations; he was gives prominence in inheritance also. But the question was if a person dies without a male child but with property? According to *Vesnusmrti,* if a person has only a daughter and no son, the daughter should be treated as son. Such a daughter is called *Putrika*. *Mitaksara* gives recognition to the son of *putrika*also. In ancient days Yaska had noted that *Putrika*was a member of her father's family (not her husband's family) because she was married with the hope that her son would belong to him (*Putrika's* father).

Evidently, the *Rajatrangini* provides us an example where in an only daughter was substituted for a son an even her name was changed for that of a male, in this connection. Dr. Shakuntala Rao Shatri quotes sacred laws and brings to our notice the prevalence of this peculiar custom in Kashmir till 9th century A.D. According to prof. Jolly, as quoted by Dr. Shatri when reading the *Ranjatarangini*, the well known history of Kashmir, with a Kasmirian, he was still living in Srinagar at the time had changed the name of his only child, a daughter, into the corresponding masculine from in order to obtain through her the same religious advantages as if she had been a son. The historical instance of the same practice in the *Rajatarangini* by which the pandits narrative of princess Kalyanadevi of Ganda, whose name was converted by her royal father into the male from Kalyanamall, makes it certain that the custom of substituting by means of a peculiar legal fiction female issue for male, where the latter was wanting is of considerable antiquity in some parts of India.[48]

Whatever may be the view of the Dharmasastra and the Smritis on the law of inheritance for women, we find a good number of cases in Kashmir of women inheriting the property either through succession or through a deed. From the *Rajatrangini* we find that women had the right to private property and they also inherited their dead husband's property. Ksemendra also speaks of a widow (though only fiction) inheriting the property of her late husband with the order from the King.[49] Dr. S.C. Ray has drawn our attention to very significant fact in this context. To put it in his own words "Women in Kashmir probably had some proprietary rights and independent legal status. A passage from *Rajatrangini* tends to show that after the death of her husband probably the widow became heir to his immovable properties and not his sons. Another passage appears to point out that women were owners of landed estates'.[50]

REFERENCES

1. L.P. Tripathi, *Position and Status of Women in Ancient India*, p. 185.
2. A.S. Altaker, *The Position of Women in Hindu Civilization*, p. 1
3. R.T., V., 157 Queen of Samkararavarman.
4. R.T., VI. 177, Daughter of Simharaja, Married to Ksemagupta.
5. R.T., VII., 123, Queen of Samgramaraja
6. R.T., VII., 152., Daughter of Inducandra. Queen of Ananta.
7. R.T., III., Daughter of Baladitya, married to Durlabhavardhana.
8. R.T., VII. Queen of Uccala.
9. R.T., VIII, 1648, Queen of Jayasimha.
10. Dr. Kamla Chauhan, "*Cultural History of Northern India*, Delhi 1992, p. 144.
11. P.N. Bazaz, "*Daughter's of Vitasta*" Srinagar 2003, P 6.
12. A.M.Shastri, *India as seen in the kuttani-mata of Damodaragupta*, pp. 108-109.
13. *Ibid*
14. S.C. Ray, "*Early History and Culture of Kashmir*", New Delhi, 1970, p. 114.
15. Dr. Ved Kumari, "*The NilamataPurana*" Vol. I, Srinagar 1960, p. 90.
16. *Ibid.* pp. 90-91

17. Prof. L.K. Tripathi, *"Position & Status of Women in Ancient India"* Vol. II Varanasi, 1992, p. 151.
18. A.M.Shastri, *op.cit.*, p. 108.
19. P.N.K. Bamzi, *"Cultural & Political History of History of Kashmir"*, Srinagar, 1994, p. 227
20. Prof. L.K. Tripathi, *op.cit* p. 152.
21. S.C. Ray *op.s.*, pp. 114, 115.
22. Prof. L.P. Trapathi *op.cit.*, p. 153.
23. R.S. Pandith *"Rajatrangini"* New Delhi, pp. 459.
24. Prof. L.P. Trapthi *op.cit* vol. II p. 153.
25. Prof. L.P. Trapathi *op.cit* p. 152.
26. P.N. Bazaz, *"Daughters of Vitasta"* pp. 10-11.
27. Prof. L.P. Trapathi *op.cit* pp. 157-154.
28. A.M.Shastri, *op.cit.*, p 106.
29. S.C. Ray *op.cit* p. 115.
30. M.L. Kapur, *"Kingdom of Kashmir"* Jammu p. 244.
31. Bazaz., *op.cit* p. 11.
32. A.M. Shastri, *op.cit.*, p 107
33. L.K.Tripathi, *op.cit.* p. 154.
34. P.N.K. Bamzi, *op.cit.*, p. 227.
35. VandanaKaushik, *"History Today: Journal of history and Historical Archaeology"* New Delhi 2010, p. 18.
36. S.C. Ray, *"op.cit"* p. 115.
37. Prof. L.P. Trapati., *op.cit* p. 155.
38. S.C. Ray *op.cit* p. 115.
39. Prof. L.P. Trapati., *op.cit* p. 156.
40. A.M. Shastri, *op.cit.*, p. 109.
41. *Ibid.*
42. S.C. Ray – *op.cit* p. 116.
43. *Ibid.*
44. M.L. Kapur, *"op.cit.,"* p. 245.
45. R.T., VII., 1220-1728.
46. P.N. Bazaz, *op.cit*, p. 12.
47. G.D. Banerjee, *op.cit* p. 370 Calcutta, 1915.
48. Shakuntala Rao Shastri, *"Women in the Sacred Laws"*, p. 157.
49. Prof. L.P. Trapathi., op.cit., pp. 163-164.
50. S.C. Ray, *op.cit.*, p. 118.

4

Prostitution

Prostitute is a word which is looked upon by the people with a very biased attitude. People have generally a very prejudicial notion about the institution of prostitution. It is an aspect of human behavior, the sexual aspect, which includes the sale of sex by a woman.

The discussion about the status of women is incomplete without the discussion about this institution. As was the case in other parts of the world, the trade of the prostitution has been practiced in India from a very early period.

Prostitutes has been in existed from the dawn of history in all countries and in the absence of statistics it is difficult to say whether it flourished more in one country than in another or whether it existed to a greater or lesser extent in ancient days as compared with modem India.[1] Prostitutes are called *Ganika, Vesya*[2], *Kuttani, Rupajiva Ksudra, varavadh, panya-vadhu*, panya-*stri, prakata-rama, dasi, vilasini, cetika, vesr-vilasavati, vare-stri, vara-ramani, sula, aniyata-pumsa, rati-silpa-jivivika* & *Abhisarika* in ancient Indian sources.[3] Some of these terms are significant as much as they throw light on some fundamental aspects of this profession. Thus, the words *rup-ajiva* and *rati-slipa-jivika* point to the fact that physical charms were the principal means of their livelihood. *Aniyata-pumsa* and words beginning with *vara* show that a harlot was not confined to any single man but was accessible to all. *Panya-stri* and *panya-vadhu* indicate that she was something like an object of trade which could be had at a fixed payment. *Dasi* and *Cetika* suggest that in the estimation of people their social status was no better than that of female slaves or manual servants. Their low social position is also suggested by the word *ksudra*. Other words indicate their luxurious life and their residence in a particular area of a town.[4]

Courtesans were recognized as a separate and special class in society as early The Vedic period. From the *Rig-Veda* we find that there were women who were common to several men i.e. who were courtesans or prostitutes. In *Rig-Veda* the bight *Marutas*(storm gods) are said to have become associated with a young courtesan[5] *ganika* (in the Ramayana) is used for the professional courtesan whose main vocation was singing and dancing. In *Mahabharata* courtesans are an established institution. The Adiparva narrates how a *Vesya* waited upon Dhrtrastra when his wife Gandhari was expecting a baby. In the Udyograparvan Yudisthira sends greeting to the *Vesyas* of the Kuravas.[6] Gautama also refers to prostitution. In the *Arthasastra* courtesans are described as an established institution. Kautliy are commends the appointment of the *Ganikadhyaksha*, i.e. Superintendent of prostitutes who watched their activities and looked- after their welfare. The prostitutes also paid regular tax to the king and attended his court and rendered him personal service[7] Kautilya also mentions that *rupajivas* would attend the harem with personal cleanliness affected by afresh bath and with fresh garments and ornaments. Narada says that intercourse is permitted with wanton women (*svairini*) who are not Brahmans by caste, with a prostitute a female slave or a female not restrained by her maser. If these belong to a caste lower than oneself; but it is forbidden with women of higher caste. In the *jatakas* also there are numerous references to prostitutes which indicate that they were tolerated and even esteemed to a certain degree. The stories of Ambapali and Salavati show the important role of the prostitutes played in the social life. Manu prohibits a Brahman from taking food offered by harlots and demands the king to punish the clever harlots. In fact prostitutes were looked down upon as degraded beings, as testified by the *Manusmriti* which places the prostitutes and gamblers with thieves and blackmailers. Kalidas also refers to prostitution[8]. The *Kamasutra* of Vatsyana defines a *ganoka* as a *vesys* who is most accomplished and proficient in the sixty four arts. They are known for their exploitative character. But in spite of this they had a recognized social status in ancient India and were not treated as outcastes or something undesirable Indian literature, whether Sanskrit, Buddhist or Jain, provides glimpses of their life. The *smritis* and *Puranas* lay down rules of conduct for prostitutes.[9] Prostitution was thus a recognized institution. Kashmir was no exception to this institution.

The main source of our information are well known texts, the *Kuttanimatam* of eighth century A.D. composed by Damodragupta, a minister of King Jayapida of Kashmir and *Samayamatrike* of poet Kshmendra of the same place who lived in the eleventh century A.D.

Ksemendra and Damodragupta tell us that prostitution was popular in the Kashmir society from early times. Kalhana also testifies to the gross immorality and laxity of character prevailing especially among the ladies of the palace and court.[10] Prostitution was primarily an urban institution with all the niceties of the glittering town life attached to it[11]. As against ordinary women of rustic habits, courtesans were ladies of refined manners and pleasant etiquettes. They were free and frank in their behavior and were able to entertain by various diversions like garden-parties and water-sports. They were witty and expert talkers and keen observers of human psychology. *Kalavilasa* of Ksemendra describes 64 arts known to the prostitutes. Being looted by them even kubera can become a pauper. The arts include *vesakala*[12], dancing, music, *kamaparijnanakala*, the art of enticing (*grahanakala*) the art of deceiving friends, the art of embracing, *ratikala*, the art of kissing, the art of being shameless, the art of trepidations, fanning, jealousy, weeping, perusing, trembling, pretending to die in separation, waiting to go prosperous houses, stealing, controlling anger, false quarrel with the mother, though looted a *kamuka* (sexy man) still trying to entice him so that he returns again, the knowledge of medicines and some *vasikaranamantras*, going to temples and gardens, hair dyeing, serving Bhikkhus etc.[13] They received liberal training epically in literary, and practical lore connected with their profession. The curriculum included erotic texts of Vatsyayana, Madanodaya, Dattaka, Vita, Rajaputra and others, the *Natya-sastra* of Bharata, Visakhilastresties on art, Dantilas writing, practical arts like arbori-horticulture, needle work, wood-work, metal-work and cookery and fine arts like painting cut work in leaves, music-vocal and instrumental and dance[14] The numerous reformers to courtesans in connection with the description of festivals indicate that prostitution was freely allowed in the society of the days of the *Nilamata*. The *Nilamata* does not decry the courtesans. The prominent ones of them, on the other hand, are enjoined upon to visit the king on his coronation day and take due part in the ceremonies a fact proving evidently their high political status.[15]

According to Vasyayana, Ganika is a superior type of prostitute. She could be acquainted with sixty four arts and should hand good qualities of beauty and behavior. Damodragupta was also referred to this type of prostitute. The love of prostitute is artificial, different in words and different in action. Such women are very difficult to understand.[16]

We have already referred to the royal connections of the prostitutes. They had a place in the King's palace and also the seraglios. But there was nothing new in Kashmir in this regard for we have evidence of prostitutes being in attendance of the king in Bana's *Kadambari* also like elsewhere, but in greater degree, senior bureaucrat's businessman, their adult sons and the king himself patronized prostitutes. Naturally many of them were rich, beautiful, highly sophisticated, trend setters in fashion and well mannered. Haralata is perhaps one such prostitute who commits even sati on the death of her patron.[17] Kalhana refers to many faithful prostitutes committing *sati* on the death of their masters. But the socio-economic condition of every prostitute was not always happy, enviable and respectable. They were poor, petty, quarrelsome and wretched in their living as in abundantly clear from Ksemendra's narrative as against the life described by Damodragupta according to which they lived in comfortable houses having paintings on the walls and reverting with music, Damodragupta also speaks of the colonies of prostitutes. It appears that the king used to appoint an officer called Sulapala to control the affairs of prostitutes. But this officer was generally a corrupt person. [18]Damodaragupta tells us about the stage of vesyamalati and her trainer Vikarala retired prostitute and the city of pravarapura (Srinagar) of Kashmir, the playground of *vesya* Kalavati and her adopted mother Gharghatika, a wanton women.

Vikarala of Damodragupta teaches young Malati the act of sex and false love sentiments capable to attract and satisfy a rich customer. As a practical instructor with large experience through which she had succeeded in grabbing, a large chunk from the wealth of a miser, discreet and cunning trader, as par narrative, she had succeeded in convincing. The trader that his son with whom her daughter is in love will ultimately get her entire possessions. And there upon by using her expertise and showing the straight of hand. She became successful in her task. It is she who dominates the whole theme like a heroine; Ksemendra tells us that without a dynamic mistress, success in the business of prostitution was not possible for a young prostitution.[19] Nor was it possible for her to keep her earnings safe from the lustful eyes of the associates of the prostitutes and other flesh mongers. And perhaps it was this contention because of which he described the early life of procuress Gharghatika who ultimately becomes in old age the mistress-cum-guardian of young Kalavati. She was the daughter of a lady who was employed at an inn. She had indulged in sex for the sake of money at a very tender age, and afterwards had become expert in obtaining money by using her physical charm and other tactics. She never had settled life like the prostitutes of from one place to another by changing her names and by becoming kept of people from various walks of life. Since she had the opportunity of enjoying the company of all types of people, her knowledge about the human behavior, particularly which is connected with libido, was immense.[20]

With this vast experience she appears more them the Kuttani's who are generally treated as capable to lure people projecting the beauty of their protégées and fleece their wealth. She is shown skilled enough to dodge the male bawds, enumerated above, including her sponsor the barber Kanka. The retentive of go betweens, as per Ksemendra, even included corrupt officials who encouraged youngsters to enjoy the young prostitutes and in been of that service they used to get commissions from the prostitutes in cash as well as in kind.[21] Money was the sole lord of the prostitutes. Thus *vesyas* appear to have belonged to that class of prostitutes who sold their flesh for money. Their social scale was naturally lower than those of other categories. In the *Rajatarangini* Kalhana also mentions courtesans who are naturally inclined towards extracting money from their lovers rather than being bothered about their good qualities?[22]

From harlots point of view pecuniary grain was the sole motive of their profession. Prostitution of the body was a means of their livelihood. For them love was a craft enabling them to secure a livelihood and body a trade able commodity. The whole corpus of trickeries elaborately described n the manuals dealing this institution and vividly illustrated in our poem was adopted by this class of women with the object of eking out their livelihood and amassing wealth in order that they might could not maintain themselves by any means other than trading their physique to satiate the sexual urge of licentious men, this idea is beautiful presented in a stanza which tells us that a prostitute is incapable in her childhood and old age and that if she happen to fall in genuine love in youth she can do nothing but beg.[23]

A hetaera always cared for immediate gain without bothering about the past of future. She could be easily approached if only one had wealth. Her feigned love and other accessory acts were coeval with wealth[24].

She is like a wooden puppet fitted with strings, who is always restless with chief tricks. She wears one hundred and one amulets on her body to guard against spirits.

She tries to keep herself youthful by eating, fish, onion soup, ghee and other nutritious foods. She though old tries to attract the notice of others with half covered face, breasts exposed to the gaze and disheveled hair style. She is praised in constant brawls.[25] She makes a show of love which is always false. There is non who can escape her.[26]

The prostitutes were protected by the state. If someone war found committing an offence against them, he had to pay heavy fines. Narada lays down that if a public woman after getting her fee refuses to receive the customer, she shall pay twice the amount of the fee and the same shall be imposed on a man who does not pay the stipulated fee, after having and intercourse with a *vesya*. *Matsyapurana* also mentions the similar provisions.

No doubt the interest of the state as well as the kings combined to continue the institution of prostitute. The rulers did not like any opposition against them and their business. Courtesans not only made the city attractive[27] but also adorned the royal courts by their presence besides providing the recreation to the people in various social functions; they also attended the royal courts and amused the kings and his courtiers by their superb performances. Besides dances in the royal court sometimes courtesans were engaged to help the king in taking bath, in performing nira-jana and to accompany the kings to the temples where they danced before the deities the feudatories also presented the beautiful courtesans to the king. They did so to the gain royal favor.[28]

The fees charged by the hetairai were known as *mulya, bhati* and *grakanaka*. Free paid in gold is referred to as *kanaka-bhati*. The fees had to be paid in advance. Every harlot had her fees fixed. Sometimes, however, the competition among the clients led to rise in fees. Fraud by either party in this respect was of common occurrence. There is, for example, a reference to a prostitute accepting fees from many and indulging in sexual act with one. Another stanza mentions the case of a strumpet who realized fee from one person but allowed another man to have sexual intercourse with her. Like, wise, we hear of some clients who had their carnal desires satiated but did not pay fees afterwards or otherwise deceived prostitutes. While we have references to courtesans being tried and fined for such offences by governmental or social agencies, there is no means to know if the clients were also similarly punished for fraud on their part. Perhaps they were not for once a customer left the residence of a courtesan it would be difficult to locate him unless he came for the second time[29].

A harlot was called *darika* before she launched on her profession. The initiation of maiden as a hetaera was an occasion to be celebrated. The man who had the first sexual intercourse with the initiate had to pay a very heavy fee which was within the reach of the rich alone. This was an aged-old custom and is referred to in other works[30]

The prostitutes are capable to earn only so long as they are young and attractive. Thus they always try to fleece their paramours for luxurious life in heydays and a comfortable one in the old age. The lot of prostitutes known was not good or honest in any respect. It is not applicable to those who entertain their lovers by their knowledge of fine arts and used to live a life befitting to kepts. The attempt to grab the money of their customers used to work even as cheats, etc like Gharghatika. It also indicates the increase in the number of prostitutes. Perhaps it was this fact because of which it was not possible for each and every prostitute to have a smooth earning. The increase in the number of commission seekers, etc. may be cited in support of this surmise. Probably the decline in trade, etc, had reduced number of adventurist trader-cum-visitors who generally used to visit the lot of ordinary prostitutes.[31]

Davadasis

Another institution somewhat similar to the above is that of *devedasi*- the servants of the gods. The close inter-relation between religion, temple and dance produced temple dancers attached to temples.

In the *Dharmasastras* seven classes of *dasis* are mentioned viz, (1) *Datta*, one who gives herself as a gift to temple, (2) *Vikrata*- one who sells herself for the same purpose (3) *Bhrtya*- one who offers herself as a temple servant for the prosperity of her family, (4) *Bhakta*- one who joins a temple out of devotion, (5) *Harita* – one who is enticed away, and presented to a temple, (6) *Alankara* – one who, being well trained in her profession and profusely decked, is presented to a temple by kings and noble-men (7) *Rudraganika* or *Gopika*- who receive regular wages from a temple and is employed to sing and dance[32].

Devadasi is an old institution formed by dancing girls. They were dedicated by their parents to the temples for god's service, and were regarded as a part of the normal establishment of the temples. These were appointed to serve deities in the temples. They were the singing girls whose duty was to provide instrumental and vocal music at the time of divine services in a temple. This institution developed after third century A.D. When India saw the emergence of a movement of building up a great number of monasteries and temples in the country,[33] the virgin girls were dedicated to the service of gods and goddesses; who had to lead a life of isolation from the outside world and of all earthly pleasure. But in course of time the atmosphere inside the temples were vitiated-leading-leading to the deterioration of morale of the peoples the *Devadasi* girls serving the deities of the temples became the object of attraction for the visitors to carry on romantic love intrigues ending in elopements. The *Devadasi* system had the support of princes, aristocrats and interested Brahamans of land, although gradually there developed a strong opposition against it, characterizing the systems unhealthy and immoral.

From very early literature we find references to dancing in temples. In the *Rig-Veda* the *apsaras* of the sea are described as following to soma, the long-haired ascetic with semi-divine powers, who is spoken of as being able to move on the path of the *apsaras* and *gandharvas*.

In the epics too, references to dancing is found. Actors and professional dancers are popular and the *ganika* is an important member of society where she is honored and her presence is considered auspicious[34].

The difference between a *ganika* and a *devedasi* is that a *ganika* is available to anyone who can pay for her entertainment where as a *devedasi* is only for a temple.

Kautilya also mentions *devedasi* who were connected with temples and are taught the art of music and dancing. All this shows that the tradition of *devedasi* was prevalent at the time of Kautiliya. Kalidas refers to dancing girls present in Mahakula temple of Ujjajani at the time of evening worship[35].

Their custom probably became common in the 6th century A.D., when most of the *Puranas*, containing a reference to it, seen to have been composed.[36] In the 7th century Hieun-Tsang saw numerous singing girls in the temple of the sun at Multan. I-Tsing also refers to the dancing girls who used to perform dance for the delight of the Buddhist deities. It indicates that the *Devadasi* system was also found in the monasteries it existed in Kashmir from a very early period, Kalhana mentions that king Jalauke game hundred ladies of his seraglio who were well versed in dancing and singing to serve in the temple of Jyestharudra[37]. *Devadasi* were patronised by kings, nobility and the priests. King Lalitaditya met two hereditary *Devadasis* in a jungle near the village of Suravardhana who spent their time in singing and dancing at the spot which was once the site of a temple. Later, the king married both of them and brought them to his palace.[38] While coming into with a number of instances of girls serving in the temples. A passage from the *Rajatrangini* tends to show that the system of dedicating girls to temples was prevalent during the reign of Durlabhaka Pratapaditya II. During the reign of Kalasa two dancing girls Kayya and Sahaja were attached to a temple. Kalhana himself was an eye witness of superannuated dancing women in the temples of the valley. It appears that it was incumbent by tradition on girls hailing from particular families to take up the profession of *Devadasi*.[39]

They were known as *Devadasis* because, through their art and skill, they served the god or Deva. They could not marry and were expected to spend their whole life in the service of the gods to whose life in the service of the gods to whose temples they were attached. By the passage of time however, the *Dvadasise* because corrupt and immoral, and not only the temple priests but the kings their nobles and other men of means also began to use them for their personal enjoyment. According to Alberuni, however, the kings deliberately encouraged this institution with a view to obtaining revenue from the business both as the fines and taxes.[40]

The *Rajatrangini* makes it quite clear that girls who served in the temples could be taken away for personal enjoyment by the king. Durlabhaka Pratapaditya II fell in love with married women named Narendrapraha. He was very eager to have the lady, but afraid of slander could not take her to his seraglio. Then the merchant Nona, the husband of Narendraprabha requested the king to adopt her as his queen but finding him reluctant finally said, "If even after this declaration you do not accept her, then you should take her from a temple as a dancing girl put there by me on account of her skill in dancing.

Again it was a merchant (a vaisya) who offered his wife to the king. Probably a man of upper castes would not have given his wife for another man. This again all the more proves that chastity of women was not considered that important or it was the man who prepared to given his wife to another man as if she was his property. But if she had gone on her own, her husband would have never accepted that.

Though the king did marry her after a little hesitation it is believed the children born of such a union would not have been accepted by the society, had it not been because of their own virtues. In fact in verse 40, Kalhana does refer to the blemish on the lineage which is due to the fact that king Chandrapidas mother was a divorcee baniya woman. Thus Kalhana expresses his opinion on heredity and the offspring of inter-cast marriage. Here again baniya agreed to give away his wife probably with the intention of material gains.

Though *devedasi* were respected and at times had the support of the king, yet theoretically hardly anybody wished to marry them. But in practice it was different. Not only a lay man but even the king is offered a *devedasi*. In the *kathasaritsagara* of Somadeva we find king Devasena fell in love with Unmadini- wife of a commander-in-chief. The king could not marry her because of her being married and her husband being alive. When Unmadinis husband came to know about it, he suggested to the king that he would give away his wife to a temple as a *devedasi* and then the king could marry her because in that case, he would no more be her husband and there was no sin in marrying a *devedasi*.

Though the commander-in-chief was prepared to leave his wife for the sake of the king, yet the king refused to marry somebody else's wife.

The king might have married her, had she been only a *devedasi*- maiden or a widow, but not one whose husband was alive. Sahaja a dancing girl attached to a temple was taken by prince Utkarsa as a concubine into the royal harem. It is thus evident that temple-girls, like common harlots could be taken away by the king.[41]

REFERENCES

1. P.V. Kane, "*History of Dharmesastra* "Vol. II, Part - I Bhandarkar Oriental Research Institute, Poona, 1974- p. 635.
2. *Vesya*- is a women or girl who sleeps with other men (leaving their husbands) and get the payment for kamabhoga. Kuttani is connected with *kamacara* and *vesyavrtti*.
3. Rajpal, *Women in early medieval North India*, the women press Delhi, 1972, p. 108.
4. A.M.Shastri, *India as seen in the Kuttani-mata of Damodragupta*, p. 113.
5. Saroji Gulati, *Women and society*, p. 217.
6. *Ibid*.
7. Rajpal, *Women in Early Mediaeval North India*, p. 109.
8. Rajpal, *op.cit.*, p. 109.
9. Prof. Dr. L.K. Trapathi, "*Position & Status of Women in Ancient India* Vol. II Banaras Hindu University, Varanasi, 1992, p. 159.

10. M.L. Kapur, *History and Culture of Kashmir* Trikuta Publishers, Jammu, 1976, p. 74.
11. A.M. Shastri, *op.cit.*, p. 111.
12. Changing Clothes or make up to Imitate anyone i.e. the Art of Imitation.
13. Sarla Khosala, *Ksemendra and his Times*, Delhi, 2001, p 139.
14. A.M. Shastri, *op.cit.*, pp. 111-112.
15. Dr. Ved Kumari, "*The Nilamata Purana*" J&K Academy of Art, Culture and Languages, Srinagar, 1968, p. 95.
16. Salara Khosla, *op.cit.*, p. 139.
17. Prof. L.K. Tripathi, *op.cit*, p. 100
18. *Ibid.*
19. Rajpal, *op.cit.*, pp. 100-115.
20. *Samayamatrika*, p. 75.
21. *Ibid.* pp. 75-80.
22. A.K. Majumdar, "*The Chaulukyar of of Gujarat*, p. 37.
23. A.M. Shastri, *op.cit.*, p. 114.
24. *Ibid.*
25. Sarla khosla, *op.cit.*, p. 33.
26. *ibid.*
27. B.P. Majumdar, "*Social Economic History of Northern India*", p. 370.
28. Rajpal, *op.cit.*, p. 116.
29. A.M. Shastri, *op.cit.*, p. 118.
30. *Ibid.*
31. L.K. Tripathi., *op.cit.*, Vol. I, p. 265.
32. Sarij Gulati, *op.cit.*, p. 223.
33. *ibid.*
34. Saraj Gulati, *op.cit.*, p. 223.
35. *Ibid.*
36. *ibid*
37. S.C. Ray "*Early History and Culture of Kashmir*, Muslim Manohara R. Lal New Delhi, 1970, p. 117.
38. Prof. L.K. Tripathi *op.cit.*, p. 161.
39. S.C. Ray, *op.cit.*, p. 117.
40. M.L. Kapur, "*Kingdom of Kashmir*", p. 135.
41. S.C. Ray, *op.cit.*, p. 117.

5

Education

Kashmir has been regarded as a seat of learning from olden days. There is no dying the fact that the students from India and abroad used to come here to seek higher education. Education, at any time and in any country, plays a vital role in shaping the destiny of the people. Education, here, as elsewhere, has always been accepted both as a potent means and a noble end to help and develop the traits of character in an individual. It was the function of education to encourage certain tendencies and to inhibit others, to give perfect discipline to body and the mind; in short to advance a human being towards perfection by bringing out the best in him and burning up all dross that might be his psychological inheritance.

The aim of education was considered to be the harmonious development of personality, such as to cultivate social efficiency, to develop spiritual sense, to inculcate moral sense and thereby to build up the character. Formation of character was an objective throughout. During the period of studentship a life of strict discipline and morality has been prescribed in the socio-religious literature of Kashmir. Moreover, perfect mastery over the senses was supposed to be one of the essential conditions for learning. It was so designed as to broaden the student's outlook on life, give him enlightenment, sharpen his intellect, and establish character through the development of his personality.

The education was mainly provided by schools run by Brahman households and *Mathas*. There were several references that private Brahmanical schools were encouraged by the ruling monarchs and private individuals by granting lands (*agraharas*) for the maintenance of their schools and for their own subsistence. Inscriptions record many instances of *Brahmadeya*[1] lands, free from all state taxes and enjoying in addition many immunities, granted by the state. King Yasaskara of Kashmir is credited with having made a gift of fifty-five *agaraharas* equipped with all sorts of material resources[2]. Besides the *agraharas*, epigraphs render to the donation of money, cows, grains, etc., also to such teachers. Private tutors are also referred to by Kalhana[3].

Schools in temples or *Mathas* have been a copy of Buddhist schools attached to Buddhist *Viharas*. With the introduction of Buddhism in Kashmir, education became popular. Many *Mathas* and *Viharas* which were in the beginning constructed for the Buddhists only, became the popular centres of learning for the masses. *Mathas* were primarily intended for the instruction of the pupils and laity by some great teachers in the tenets or in the doctrines of some philosophy or in some branches of learning as grammar and astronomy etc. Here *Mathas* does not appear to have any technical sense. In *Rajatrangini*, *Matha* is defined as a place where pupils reside[4]. These were residential institutions which promote higher philosophical learning and attracted students from all parts India, Tibet and china[5]. From *Rajatrangini* we come to know that innumerable *Mathas* of Brahmanas, Shaiva and Pasupata in Kashmir were established[6]. Kalhana has recorded that king Yasaskara of Kashmir built a *Matha* who went there in quest of learning[7]. According to Ksemendra the students of Bengal and Gauda went over to Kashmir to receive education in the *Mathas*[8]. Such students travelled for and wide in search of knowledge. After learning various branches of philosophy and Sanskrit works, in order to get the highest diploma they came to Kashmir[9]. *Kathasaritsagara* also refers that learned Brahmanas used to come here for discussions from distant places. Like the Buddhist *Viharas* these *Mathas* also had a temple attached to them. Temples and *Matha* have been supplementary in the period under review. Students were provided food and other facilities in these *Mathas*. In Kashmir a king donated all his wealth to *Matha* where pupils were taught. King Avantivarman of Kashmir appointed Ramata Upadhyaya to the post of expounder of grammar in a temple[10]. Many kings like Lalitaditya, Ananta, and Queen Didda of Kashmir founded several *Mathas* and *Viharas* for the residence of students.[11] It shows that *Mathas* in Kashmir were the sacred homes of high learning.

Students came to Kashmir from far off places, in spite of the long and arduous, they had to undergo, on account of the excellence of the learned teacher there, all recognised as authorities on their respective subjects. As the examination was very stiff, only few students were successful. Most of them, being rejected, wandered in the streets of Kashmir. Ksemendra has given a vivid account of such students, in every humorous style, describing their notorious character, vicious habits and customs[12] of the day. Thus it may be said that that the teachers imparted their knowledge only to those students, who had capacity for learning it.

The young students, who were selected, were governed by certain rules and had to perform certain duties during the studies. The students went to the residence of their teachers for study. It was deemed to be the duty of a student to render personal service to his teacher. Students were anxious to see their teachers happy. He had to beg daily for his alms[13]. Students were expected to do all household works[14]. In the *gurukula* he lived under the personal care and guidance of the teacher who was spiritual parent. The teacher was expected to possess the highest moral, intellectual and spiritual qualifications.

As Kashmir was the home of Vagdevi (goddess of *vidya*) it is but natural that it had good libraries and books on various subject taught here. The Vedas, Dharma-sastra texts, grammar, metrics, poetics, erotic's, medicine, philosophy and creative literature as also fine arts were more or less rigorously studied[15]. The main subjects of the study were the Vedas. The study of the Vedic texts was epically cultivated in the Brahmana families. Discussions on the divergent interpretations of Vedic passages often took place, and at least some Brahmanas were skilled reciters of Vedic hymns[16]. During the king of Samkaravarman, Kalhana describes, there was Brahman scholar who was well versed in all the four Vedas. Named Nayaka, he was placed in charge of two temples built by the king[17].

Alberuni informs us that the grammar and astronomy cum astrology were important subjects of study. Grammar was an important subject during the period under review. Grammar was hence the key to every branch of learning hence we find efficient grammarian was appointed to the office of the preacher of the temple in Kashmir[18]. Kalhana informs us that king Jayapida encouraged the study of Paninian grammar in his dominions. He brought competent grammarians from abroad and restored the study of *Mahabasya*. King Jayapida is said to have learnt Sanskrit grammar from Ksira, a master of grammatical science and gained distinction with the wise[19]. The impression thus obtained about the popularity of grammatical studies in Kashmir during the period under study is confirmed by several references.

According to Ksemendra in addition to philosophical works of various religions (Shaivism, Vaisnavism, Buddhism etc.), there existed books on astrology and astronomy. Among the two siddhantas viz, Astronomy and Astrology the later drew the attention of the people. Astrology was made one of the functionaries of the state[20] and an honourable number of the royal court who had no such position in the early periods.

The *Silpasthanavidya* (arts and crafts) was compulsory subject at Buddhist universities. The proper and exhaustive training given in the subject is attested to by the architectural remains and sculptures belonging to the period. The story of Suyya probably tends to suggest traditions concerning the studies in engineering. He is credited with the construction of dams etc. to control the floods in Kashmir[21]. Kalhana refers to the training of merchants and clerks under a teacher. According to him, 'courtesans, the officials (Kayastha) and the clerk (divira) and the merchants being (all) deceitful by nature are (in this respect) superior to a poisoned arrow that they have been trained under a teachers advice[22].

Damodragupta describes, the curriculum in the 9th century A.D. included sexual sciences of Vatsyayana, Dattaka, Vitaputra and Rajaputra, the *Natyasastra* of Bharata, Visakhilas treatise on art, Dantilas work on music, *Vrksayurveda*, painting, needlework, woodwork, metal work, clay modelling, cookery, and practical training in instrumental music, singing, and dancing[23].

REFERENCES

1. A piece of land granted by the king to a teacher was known as *brahmadeya*.
2. R.T*., VI. 89.
   *R.T. = KALHAN'S RAJATRANGINI, Translated by M.A. STEIN.
3. R.T., V 78.
4. R. T., VI 87, 88.
5. Dr. Kaul, *Educational Studies and Investigation* (journal) Vol. 1.
6. R.T., IV 512, 696, V 38, 244, 245, VI, 87, 88, 99, 104, 300. 305. 307, VII, 120, 242, 149, 180, 183, 214, 608, 961, 1678.
7. R.T., VI 87.
8. Sarla Khosla, *Ksemendra and his times*, p. 170
9. *Ibid.*
10. R.T., V. 29.
11. R.T. V 28, 29.
12. Sarla Khosla, *op.cit.*, p 170. Sometimes such students were expelled from the Mathas.
13. A.M Shastri., *India as seen in the Kuttanimata of Damodaragupta.*, p. 171.
14. *ibid.*
15. A.M Shastri., *op.cit.*, p. 172.
16. *Ibid.* p. 174.
17. R.T., V., 159.
18. R.T., V. 29.
19. R.T., VI 488, 489.

20. R.T., I., 119.
21. R.T., V. 78.
22. R.T., VIII. 131.
23. S.C .Ray., *Early History and Culture of Kashmir.*, p. 114.

6

Religion

Naga Worship

The Naga worship seems to have been established in the valley from a remote period and undoubtedly has been one of the earliest religions of the land. In Kashmir, the people have shared the belief that snakes live in springs. They also believed that snakes could appear in human form, marry and have children[1]. A spring is called a Nag in Kashmir even today. The earliest inhabitants of the valley cherished aboriginal beliefs, among which the snake cult was popular.

The Naga worship prevailed in early Kashmir receives confirmation not only from the accounts of Ceylon, China, and Tibet but also from native literature. The *Nilamatapurana* informs us that the valley of Kashmir called *Satidesa* was occupied in ancient times by the Nagas only. Regarding the origin of Nagas it is stated that they were the progeny of Prajapati Kasyapa and his wife Kadru – the daughter of Daksa[2]. *Nilamatapurana* narrates how Kashmir was created out of water and left to the care of Nagas of whom Nila, the son of Reshi Kashap was the chief. The Nagas are supposed to reside in the springs and lakes and from early times considerable importance had been attached to their worship. The long account on Nagas given in the *Nilamatapurana*, the numerous temples built near the more famous springs, and the popularity and undoubtedly ancient origin of the pilgrim – ages directed to the latter, show the deep seated belief in

Nagas worship among the people of the valley[3]. Even the names of places like, Verinag, Anantnag etc. shows the traces of ancient Naga beliefs.

Hiuen Tsang who visited valley during the reign of Durlabhavardhana refers to the Nagas many a times. According to Hiuen Tsang Kashmir was originally a dragon lake[4]. Abul Fazal informs us that there were in Kashmir seven hundred places to serpent's[5].even now Naga worship exists in some form or the other in Kashmir and other parts of India[6].

The *Mahavamsa* narrates that it was during the reign of Ashoka that Majhantika was deputed to Kashmir, which was under the rule of the Naga king, Aravala, who could destroy the corn and other harvest by hailstorm. Majhantika was met with hail and rain on his approach to Kashmir, but due to his divine powers he remained unaffected, by this. The Naga king realised his spiritual powers and together with his followers submitted before the monk and accepted Buddhism[7]. His journey to Kashmir has also been narrated in Kashmir sources. The Nagas were eminently popular deities in the happy valley is also testified to by Kalhana's *Rajatrangini*. According to Kalhana Kashmir was a land protected by Nila, the lord of all Nagas, who was worshiped at Verinag[8].

Nilamatapurana, describes that Nagas received worship on many festivals. The Nila was worshiped on the first snowfall. Nila as well as the local Nagas were to be worshiped with offerings of flowers and fruits[9]. Nila and Nagas were also worshiped on the *Iramanjaripujana* festival along with other gods and goddess[10]. Another ceremony called *Varunpancami* was held on the fifth day of Bhadra and was connected with the worship of serpent king Nila[11]. Kalhana narrates that during the reign of Abhimanyu Kashmir witnessed severe winter for a number of years in succession. This occurrence came in handy to the Nagas and the Brahman Clergy. They said perhaps from sincere belief – that the excessive snowfalls had been brought about by the Naga gods, who had been displeased by the stoppage of the customary offerings to them[12]. Then a Brahaman named Candradeva, who was descended from Kasyapa, practised austerities to please Nila – the lord of the Kashmir and protector of the land- and when the affliction of excessive snowfall came to an end, it was ascribed by them to the gracious intervention of Nila[13]. The revival of Naga cult was the tremendous hard work by Candradeva. According to *Rajatrangini*, Durlabhaverdhana, the founder of Karkota dynasty was son of Karkota Naga[14]. Kalhana mentions that a great annual festival was celebrated in honour of the Naga king Taksaka, frequented by dancers and strolling players, and thronged by crowds of spectators[15].

Buddhism

Kashmir is known as the paradise on earth. It has been acclaimed as a land of bliss, peace and contentment. It may be noted that after its exile from the place of its birth, Buddhism found its refuge in Kashmir. "The influence of Kashmir was very marked, especially in the spread of Buddhism beyond India. From Kashmir it penetrated into Qandahar and Kabul and thence over Bactria: Tibetan Buddhism has also its essential origin from Kashmir; so great is the importance of this region in the history of this religion".

The history of Buddhism in Kashmir has not been much different than its history in the rest of the country. When it came it harbingered its doctrine of love, piety, universal brotherhood, spiritual discipline, high morals, equality and liberty for all classes and for both sexes. When did actually the spread of Buddhism start in Kashmir? Historians have various theories and ideas. It is commonly believed that Buddhism came to Kashmir in the region of Ashoka. But that is not correct. The new faith had travelled to happy valley much earlier. Buddhism was prevalent in Kashmir in the time of the native king Surrendra[16]. He belonged to a dynasty whose members are known for their religious endowment. His father Khagendra had created two such endowments, one of them having left its name to the existing village of Khoamuh near Pampore. True to the family tradition,

Surrender erected the first *Vihara* at Soura in Kashmir[17]. His reign can be fixed in the middle of the Ist century B.C[18]. Kalhana says that there were *Viharas* in Kashmir before Ashoka. Moreover we are told that Ashoka invited Buddhist missionaries from Kashmir to participate in his religious council[19]. It is thus clear that there existed Buddhism in Kashmir before the reign of Ashoka. *Nilmatapurana* testifies the existence of Buddhism in Kashmir side by side with Naga cult and Vaisnavism. *Nilmatapurana* describes the celebration of Buddha's birthday with great rejoicing in the bright half of the month of vaisakha. Buddha's *Caityas* were decorated with beautiful paintings and Buddha's images were offered water, scents, flowers and jewels. For three days worship continued with the chanting of holy verses[20].

According to *Mahavamsa*, Ashokas adviser, Moggaliputta Tissa sent his missionary Majjhantika to peach Buddhism in Kashmir and Gandhara[21]. Majjhantika won over the ruler and the people of that region on account; it is said, of his supernatural powers[22]. The history of the mission of Majjhantika receives confirmation from traditions recorded in the Tibetan work Dul-va and the account of Hieun T sang[23]. It is reported that Madhyantika brought with him many Bhiksus for settlement and he himself remained in the valley for nearly 20 years[24]. This very Buddhist preacher is supposed to have introduced the forming and also the cultivation of world famous Saffron in the valley.[25]

We learn from Kalhana that Kashmir formed a part of the empire of Ashoka who was follower of "Jina" I.e. Buddha[26]. Kalhana depicts Ashoka as a propagator of religious tolerance. He allowed the people to practice their own religion and follow their own customs and traditions. However he directed his missionaries to propagate his faith of Buddhism. Many Kashmir's readily accepted the four Noble truths and eight rules of right conduct propounded by Buddhism. The emperor built numerous *stupas* and *chaityas*. Four of his *stupas* even existed at the time of Hieun Tsangs visit to the valley in the middle of the 7th century[27]. These are said to have contained

Buddhas relics[28]. Ashoka built two Buddhist *stupas* at Hukalitar and Vethavutur, in Badgham and Anantnag. Vethavutur is regarded as the source of the rive Jehlum in Kashmir. Buddhist relics, such as statues have been found at the older site of Srinagar, Pandrathan, and Huklitar. Some of the statues have been brought to the government museum, Srinagar[29]. The important contribution of king Ashoka was that he laid the foundation of the city of Shrinagari identified at the site of the present Pandrethan (Kalhana's Purandhisthana)[30]. The great emperor, who was zealous always in preaching and disseminating the religion of Buddha throughout the length and breadth of his kingdom and even beyond, seems to have tried his best to spread it in the secluded vale of Kashmir too.[31] Historically speaking Asoka inaugurated the Buddhism in Kashmir when he brought 5,000 Buddhist monks and settled them in Kashmir to popularize the Hinayana Buddhism in Kashmir and adjacent territories. He built several *Mathas*, as he thought Kashmir was an ideal place for pursuing higher studies and spiritual practices.

Asoka was successes by his son Jaloka[32]. It is said that he was not favourable to Buddhism in the beginning[33]. At the instance of Avadhuta, he took a vow that he would follow only Shaivism[34]. He persecuted the Buddhists, and destroyed their *Viharas* ans *Stupas*[35]. But subsequently at the request of Kritya he modified his attitude and later became more friendly towards them and constructed a big *Vihara*, the Krityashrama, in the vicinity of Baramulla[36].

Menander, who is believed to have ruled towards the end of the second and in the beginning of the first century B.C., was a great scholar and inquirer after truth. He came under the influence of Buddhism. It goes to the credit of Nagasena, to have defeated Menandera in a religious discussion which was held at a place which was only 12 yojnas from Kashmir[37] and as a result of this discussion Menander embraced Buddhism and became Arhat[38]. Their conversations form the subject matter of the celebrated Sanskrit work *Milindapanha*. He built a *Vihara* which was named after him as *Milindevihara*[39].

With the coming of Kushanas, Buddhism received a tremendous support. There is no dying the fact that during their rule, Buddhism enjoyed royal patronage. Kalhana in his *Rajatrangini* provides historical evidence about the three Kushana rulers, Hushka, Juska, and Kanishka[40]. Each one of the founded here a town after his name, and these were called Huskapura, Juskapura, and Kaniskapura respectively[41]. These Kushana kings were given to acts of piety and built many *Viharas, Mathas, Caityas* and similar other structures[42]. Amongst these Kanishka is most famous. From the time of Kanishka, the Buddhism of Kashmir entered its golden phase during the reign of Kanishka. He donated the valley to Buddhists. This brought and gathered Buddhist students from all over the country and the world at large[43]. According to a Buddhist tradition, the king Kanishka, on the advice of Parshva convened a Buddhist council in Kashmir[44]. The objective of the council was to prepare commentaries on the canons[45]. The council which sat for six months, collected all available sayings and teachings of the Buddha and other masters of the law and drew up expository commentaries on the *Sutra* (sermons), the *Vinaya* (discipline) and the *Abhidharma* (metaphysics)[46]. The treatises written on copper plates had been enclosed in stone boxes and deposited in a *Stupa* made especially for the purpose[47]. Besides large audience, this council was attended by500 Arhatas, 500 Bodhisattvas and 500 Panditas[48]. Asvaghosa, the celebrated author of the *Buddhacarita*, the *Saundrananda* and the *Sariputraprakarna* attended this council[49]. The credit also goes to this council that first time in the history of Buddhism, freedom of thought and expression was recognized and it was declared that the texts of all the 18 schools of thought in Buddhism were correct, for all of them contained the world of the master. The council is also important henceforth Kashmir became the headquarters of Sarvastivdin school of Buddhism[50], which was popularized by the Kashmiri's in central Asia, Tibet, china and south East Asia. Vairochana was the Kashmirian missionary, built the first Buddhist *Vihar* at Khotan in the central Asian region[51].

Kalhana describes the illustrious Buddhist philosopher Nagarjuna who lived in Kashmir in the time of the Kushanas as 'the sole supreme ruler of the land'[52]. It was due to his knowledge that the Buddhists of Kashmir maintained their ascendancy over the acharayas[53].

According to Kalhana, Kushana kings in Kashmir were followed by Abhimaniyu[54], in whose reign Buddhism received a check in Kashmir. Buddhism received a great setback during the reign of Nara. He was a great enemy of Buddhism. He burnt thousands of Buddhist *Viharas*, and granted the villages which had belonged to them, to Brahmans[55].

The next important king of Kashmir was Mihirkula[56]. He was a great persecutor of Buddhists. He pulled down Buddhist monasteries of northern India and massacred the monks[57]. Meghavahana is said to have been a kind hearted man as he prohibited slaughter of animals in his kingdom[58]. He was a Buddhist and tried to revive the dying faith. His queen Amrtaprabha erected a lofty *Vihara* called Amrtabhavana for the benefit of Bhiksus[59]. Kalhana compare the king with Jina i.e, Buddha[60]. There is mention of the erection of a big *Vihara* during the reign of Pravarasena by his uncle Jayendra known as *Jayendravihara*[61]. This *Vihara* was visited by Hiuen Tsang during his stay in Kashmir. Jayendra also erected a Buddhist statue[62].

According to the *Rajatrangini*, Durlabhvardhana, was the first ruler of Karkota dynasty[63]. Hiuen Tsang visited Kashmir during his reign. Hiuen Tsang has given valuable information about the large number of Buddhist monasteries existing at that time. Then the illustrious king Lalitaditya became the ruler of Kashmir[64]. During the days of Lalitaditya three faiths flourished side by side in Kashmir. The king hence built temples of Vishnu and Siva and Buddhist *Viharas* as well as *Stupas*[65]. The king also built the wonderful and famous *Rajavihara*, with a large quadrangle (catuhsala), a large Caitya, and a large image of Buddha[66]. At Parihasapura, Chankuna, a Tukhara minister of the king erected the Chankunavihara, built a *Stupa* and placed there golden image of Jina, i.e.,

Buddha[67]. Chankunas brother in law Ishanachandra who was a royal physician also built a *Vihara* with a number of golden images of Buddah[68]. Tantric Buddhism[69] seems to have been developed in this period. Chanakuna his minister is credited as Tantric Buddhist[70]. Jayapida[71], the grandson of Lalitaditya came to the throne in 751 A.D. The king was a liberal patron of learning, and many poets and scholars flocked his court[72]. He worshipped both Vishnu and Buddha. King Jayapida is said to have built *Viharas* and Hindu temples at Andarkot a mile away from the village of Sumba, near the entrance of Manasbal Lake. At present practically everything is destroyed[73].

Buddhism seems to have been overshadowed by the growing Vaisnava and Saiva faith which became predominant in the valley in the centuries following the Karkota period. Avantivarman laid the foundation of Utpala dynasty in 855[74] A.D. He heralded a new era in the history of Kashmir. He was a rare combination of strength and gentleness, and the first and most conscientious servant of the state. Avantivarman was a staunch follower of Siva and Vishnu. During his reign Kashmir witnessed a great rise in the popularity of Shavism. This was due to the fact that some of the greatest philosophers of Kashmir Shavism lived about this time. One of them, Bhatta Kallata is mentioned by Kalhana in Avantivarmans time[75]. Henceforth the masses were attracted towards Saivaism. Avantivarman showed great regard for Buddhism also and prohibited the killing of all living beings[76]. His pious engineer Suyya, who was also a Vaishnava, latter issued a prohibition against the killing of fishes in the Vitasta. Avantivarman was succeeded by his son Shankarvarma[77]. During this period Buddhism was in a decayed condition. Shankarvarma, either confiscated lands and *Viharas* or plundered these shrines[78]. Shankaravarman's queen Sugandha was killed in a monastery, called Nispalaka *Vihar*[79].

During the reign of Kshemagupta[80] (A.D 950-9580) Kashmir saw one of the worst periods of her history. He was a great Shiva worshiper. Kalhana describes that Kshemagupta burnt down a Buddhist *Vihara* named *Jayendravihar*[81]. From this decaying *Vihara* he took away the brass image of *Sugata* Buddha and utilized the stones of *Jayendravihara* for erecting a Shiva temple in his own name[82]. He confiscated thirty- six villages which belong to the burnt *Vihara* and gave them to Khasa ruler[83]. Kshemaguptas reign is important in the history of Kashmir by reason of his mirage to Didda[84]. Didda so much dominated the mind of the king that he nick named *Diddaksema*[85]. She founded a number of temples and other sacred buildings. She is started to have made sixty four foundations of which, *Diddamatha* has given its name Didamar to a locality in Srinagar (on the right bank of the Vitasta). She restored some of the buildings and enclosed with stone walls almost all the temples whose walls had been burnt down. She also repaired the *Jayendravihara*. Didda died o 1003 A.D.

Between 1003-1101A.D., Buddhism degenerated and lost the royal patronage. Buddhist nuns and monks lost high ideas of morality. The works of Ksemendra and Somendra bear ample testimony[86].

According to a version Buddhism, had led the country of Kashmir in awakening the common people and arousing a spirit of defiance in the against obscurantism and social injustice. A dynamic society of freedom had taken birth which was absorbed in making original contribution to philosophy, literature, arts, architecture and science. From here spread Buddhism beyond Himalayan countries. Its wandering monks took philosophical ideas beyond its borders to Ladakh, Tibet, Khotan, china, etc. All these are indebted to Kashmir for Buddhism, Buddhist literature and civilization.

Shavism

Kashmir remained under the yoke of Hindu and Buddhist rulers till the 14th century A.D. under these kings the various sects of Hinduism (Shavism, Vashinuism, and Tantracism) and various forms of Buddhism (Mahayana and Vayrayana) got impetus to rise and flourish together and peacefully.

Shiva worship as a popular faith had been prevalent in Kashmir from a remote age[87]. If Kalhana is to be believed Shavism must have been the predominant religion in Kashmir long before Buddhism was introduced. There was a shrine of Shiva Vijayesa even in Ashokan days[88]. Shavism and Buddhism flourished side by side in Kashmir during Ashokas time and received the Emperors patronage in almost equal measures. Ashoka not only replaced the stuccoed enclosure of Shiva's shrine by new stones but also built two Shiva temples at the ancient site of Vijayeshvara (Bijbehara) and named both after his own name as Asokesvara[89]. Ashoka's son Jalauka was an ardent Shaivist and made vow that he would ever worship Shiva Vijayesvara and Jyesthesa residing at Nadisaksetra[90]. He also erected a shrine of Jyestharudra at Srinagar[91]. The king built a stone temple at Nandiksetra for Shiva Bhutesa[92]. Then a king named Damodara-II, who was descended from Ashoka's race, ruled the earth[93]. He is said to have been crest jewel of Shiva worshippers[94].

After a dozen local kings, Kashmir came into the possession of king Mihirakula[95]. Himself being a devotee of Shiva, he let loose the violence and the disaster of the Buddhist structures in the valley. He founded the shrine of Shiva Mihiresvara at Srinagar[96]. According to the chronicle, the king lavished his generosity by granting a thousand *agraharas* to the Brahman's of Gandharan at Vijayesvara[97]. Mihirakulas son Baka constructed the shrine of Shiva Bakesa[98]. Gopaditya, prominently stands out for his patronage of Shavism and the Brahman's, built a new temple Jyestheshvara, on the Shankaracharya hills in Srinagar. He also bestowed the Gopa *agrahara's* on Brahmans born in Aryadesa[99]. His son Narendraditya-I, also known as Khinkhila, constructed the shrine of Shiva Bhutesvara[100], and his Guru, Ugra, constructed the temple of Shiva Urgesa[101]. According to Kalhana, Tunjina and his pious wife Vakpushta sustained the land nobly with its various castes. These two rulers built the temple of Shiva called Tungesvara[102]. King Sresthasena, also known as pravarasena-I, constructed the first shrine of Pravaresvara[103], and king Pravarasena-II, who was ardent worshiper of Shiva[104], built the linga of Pravaresvara[105]. Another king Ranaditya is said to have erected temples and shrines in Honour of Shiva[106].

During the reign of Karkota rulers, several important and beautiful temples have been erected for Shiva worship. Lalitaditya Muktapida's mother Narendraprabha built a Shiva temple called Narendresvara after her own name[107].during the days of Lalitaditya people followed three faiths side by side. The king hence built temples of Vishnu, Shiva and Buddhist *Viharas* and *Stupas*. Lalitaditya erected a lofty temple of stones for Shiva Jyestharudra and made a grant of land and villages for the maintenance of the temple[108]. His minister Mitrasarman built the Shiva Linga called Mitresvara[109]. Acharya Bhappats built the temple of Shiva called Bhappatesvara. Many other shrines of Shiva called Rakchatera etc. were put up by a host of people[110]. King Jayapida built a shrine of Shiva Acesvara[111].

In Avantivarman's time Kashmir witnessed a great rise in the popularity of Shavism. This was due to the fact that some of the greatest philosophers of Kashmir Shavism lived about this time. One, of them Bhatta Kallata is mentioned by Kalhana as living in Avantivarmans time[112]. Bhatta Kallata is known as the pupil of Vasugupta who was the founder of Spandasastra branch of Kashmir Shaiva philosophy. The fillip which Shavism got as a result of the efforts and expositions of these great masters made it the foremost faith in the valley for centuries to come and threw into shade both Vaishnuism and Buddhism. King Avantivarman founded at Avantipura, the temple of Avantisvara in honour of Lord Shiva and also fitted pedestals with silver conduits at the Shiva shrine of Tripuveswara, Bhutesh and Vijayesa[113]. Avantivarmans minister Sura, his wife Kavyaderi and his son Ratnavardhana were all devotees of Shiva. Sura built temple of Suresvara at Survariksetra in honour of Shiva[114]. His son Ratnavardhana built a temple of Shiva Bhutesvara[115].

Avantivarman was succeeded by his son Samkaravarman[116]. He was a devotee of Shiva. In company with his queen Sugandha, he built temples of Shiva Samkaragaurisa and Sugandhesa[117]. Shiva was worshiped with great devotion not only in Karkota and Utpala period, but also in the succeeding ages. King Parvagupta founded the Shrine of Shiva Parvaguptesvara near the site of the Skandabhavanavihara[118]. Ksemagupta erected the temple of Shiva Ksemagaurisvara[119].

In 1003A.D. Samgramaraja became king and inaugurated the rule of the first Lohara dynasty[120]. Samgramaraja is said to have obtained religious merit by restoring the illustrious shrine of Shiva Ranesvara[121]. Queen Suryamati founded the temple Of Shiva Gaurisvara, and constructed the meritorious Subhatamatha on the bank of the *Vitasta*[122]. She also granted under her husband's name *agraharas* at Amaresvara, and arranged for the consecration of Trisulas, Banalingas and other sacred emblems[123]. Her husband Ananta, was also a devotee of Shiva, he surpassed even the Munis by his devotion to Shiva[124]. Ananta's son Kalasa restored the famous stone temple of Vijsyeswara which had been damaged by fire[125]. He also built the Shiva temples of Tripuresvara and Kalasesvara[126]. All these temples were adorned with golden parasols, cups and the like.

Under the second Lohara dynasty, Shavism continued to flourish. During the reign of king Jayasimha, his minister Rilhana, built the shrine of Shiva Rihanesvara at Puranadhisthana[127]. Similarly his other ministers also built temples in honour of Lord Shiva.

The Kashmir Shavism has two branches, the Spandasastra and Pratyabhijasastra. The authorship of the first is attributed to Vasugupta and his pupil Kallata. The two principle works of the system are the Sivasutram or Sivasutrani and the Spandakarikas. The Sutras are said to have been revealed to Vasugupta by Shiva himself[128]. These he taught to his disciples as Shiva Sutras. One of his brilliant student Bhatta Kallata, composed these teachings as Spandakarikas[129]. The founder of the Pratyabijna school of Kashmir Shavism was Somananda. It is called pratyabijna, because according to it release of the individual soul depends on the recognition (pratyabhijna) of its identity with Shiva[130]. The work written by Somananda is called Sivadrsti. But the principal treatise of the school was composed by his pupil Udayakara, and contains verses which are called Sutras[131].

These philosophical treaties were further developed in the subsequent century by Shiva scholars like Utpala Deva, Mokul Raj, Indu Raj and Rama Kant, who wrote extensive commentaries on the subject. The philosophy reached the climax under the scholarship of saint Abhinav gupta, who lived in Kashmir, during the end of the 10th and the beginning of 11th century A.D.[132] To him goes the credit of giving the proper shape to the Shiva philosophy spread in different works. Abinava gupta wrote commentaries on Utpalacharya's works, on the *Para- Trimshika* (Tantra) and composed the great work *Tantraloka* which is an independent treatise and the *Tantrasara*, besides numerous other works[133]. *Tantraloka* throws sufficient light on the practical Yoga as well as the fundamental tenants of monistic Shiva philosophy and expands the whole system of Kashmir Shavism.

Vaishnavism

Though the origin of Vashnuism in Kashmir cannot be traced, it can safely regarded as one of the oldest cults of thee valley. Vaishnuism occupies an important place in the *Nilamatapurana* which speaks of Vishnu more than any other deity[134]. The *Nilamatapurana*, like other *Vaishnupuranas*, describe Vishnu as the highest, god, praised and honoured even by Brahman and Shiva[135]. It attaches so much importance to the faith as to make Buddha as an incarnation of Vishnu[136]. Side by side with Buddhism and Shavism, the cult of Vaishnuism also flourished in Kashmir during the Hindu period. Parvaasena-II is recorded to have consecrated the image of Vishnu Jayaswamin[137]. Another image of Vishnu Ranas- Jayaswamin, was built by king Ranaditya[138].

Under the rule of Karkota dynasty Vashnuism not only received royal patronage but seem to have been popular among the people. Durlabhavardhana, the founder of Karkota dynasty consecrated at Srinagar the shrine of Vishnu Durlabhasvami[139]. A son of the king Malhana built the Shrine of Vishnu Malhanasvamin[140]. King Chandrapida built the shrine of Vishnu Tribhuvanasvamin[141]. His Guru, a man of noble virtues, called Mihiradatta, built the temple of Gambhirasvamin[142]. His city-perfect, called Chalitaka, built the temple of Vishnu Chalitasvamin[143].

Like Ashoks Lalitaditya extended his patronage to all the faiths prevalent in the valley, in his time. The king hence built temples of Vishnu and Shiva and Buddhist *Viharas* as well as *Stupas*. He was a great devotee of Vishnu. When he had resolved (Krtaniscaya) upon the conquest of the world, he built the town called, "suniscitapura', feeling proud, he built Darpitapura with a shrine of Kesava Vishnu[144]. At Huskapura he built the splendid shrine of Vishnu Muktasvamin[145]. After constructing at Lokapunya a town, which was provided with the requisite accessories, the victorious king made it, together with villages, an offering to Vishnu[146]. In the town of Parihasapura, which the king constructed in honour of his adored deity, he built the glorious silver image of Vishnu, Parihasakesava[147]. At Huskapura, the glorious silver image Vishnu Muktakesava, was made out of gold[148]. A fourth one, that of boar incarnation of Lord Vishnu, Mahavaraha[149]. He also consecrated two images of Vishnu, one under the title of Govardhanadhara[150] and the other of Ramasvamin[151], the latter near the temple of Parihasakesa.

Lalitadiysa's zeal for foundations of Vishnu temples, Shrines and Statues, was perhaps responsible for similar works of his queen, ministers and courtiers. His queen Kamalavati put up a large silver image of Kamalakesava[152]. His minister Mitrasarman, built the famous shrine of Vishnu, Kayyasvamin[153]. Some of the late Karkota kings also patronised Vaishnuism. The king Jayapida worshiped both Vishnu and Buddha[154]. His mother, Amrtaprabha, built the temple of Amrtaesava for the deliverance of her dead son[155].

Vaishnuism received further impetus under the reign of Avantivarman. He built the temple of Vishnu Avantisvamin, even before his accession to the throne[156]. His brother, Suravarman founded a temple of Suravarmasvamin and a Gokula[157]. Samara, another brother of king, founded for Kesava in his quadruple from a temple called Samarasvamin[158]. The illustrious Mahodaya, who was the chief door-keeper of Sura, consecrated the shrine of Vishnu Mahodayasvamin, and gave that temple the post of recite (Vyakhyatr) to a teacher called Ramata, who was famous for his labours on grammatical science[159]. His engineer Suyya, was also an ardent Vaishnu. He built at the new confluence of the Sindhu and Vitasta atemple of Hrsikesa Yogasayin[160].

The popularity of Vaishnuism in the eighth century is further attested by the discovery of several images of Vishnu in his different Avatrars throughout the length and breadth of the valley, particularly at Verinag, Martand, Avantipura, Baramula and Andar-kot[161].

The development of Vaushnuism in Kashmir, from the 10th century onwards, is evidenced from Kalhana's *Rajatrangini*, queen Sugandha built the town of Gopalapura, the Gopalamatha and the temple of Vishnu Gopalakesava[162]. Nanda, the wife of Gopalavarman, founded the temple of Nandakesava[163]. From the tenth century to the end of the Hindu rule in the 14th century we find several kings and queens founding temples and shrines.

Minor Deites

Walled off by high mountains and endowed with unequalled natural beauty. Kashmir remained an inviolate sanctuary of Indian culture, till the 14th century Buddhism, Shavism, and Sanskrit learning flourished in the valley and produced a remarkably rich culture till the Muslim conquest overturned the social structure the evidence at our disposal leaves no doubt that Shavism, Buddhism and Vaisnavism flourished in ancient Kashmir. Besides these the people also worshiped numerous minor Hindu gods and goddesses irrespective of the sect to which they might have belonged. Most important of them include Surya, Karttikeya, Ganesa, Agni, and Laksmi[164].

Surya (also known as Aditya) is Brahmanical male deity, who was widely worshiped all over North India during this period[165]. He is considered the creator of the universe and the source of all life. He is the supreme soul who brings light and warmth to the world. He may be worshiped on all the seventh days of fortnights but especially on those of Margasira[166]. The god sun referred to as Hari, Patanga and Candabhas, had seven horses yoked to his chariot[167]. Horses were as important an emblem of Surya as the Kaustubha was of Vishnu and elephant of Indra[168]. Ranadatiya[169] is said have built at the village of Simharotsika a temple of Martanda which became famous everywhere under the name of Ranapurasvamin[170]. The limestone temple is an interesting example of the influence of classical architecture in the region and has fluted columns and Corinthian like capitals in the rectangular colonnade which measures 67* 42 meters and surrounds the temple proper. Today the temple is a mere ruin of its former self, but it remains the earliest Hindu monument in Kashmir. In the 8th century A.D. Lalitaditya[171] erected the shrine of Aditya at the town of Lalitapura. He built another massive stone temple of Surya under the name of Martanda[172] the ruins of which have survived. Kalhana states that king Suryavarman[173] paid homage to the temple of sun god Jaya Swamin[174]. The copper image of Surya, called Tamrasvamin was one of the most celebrated shrines of the valley in the 11th century A.D.[175] Taruna swamin temple of Kashmir was one of the most popular shrines during the period under review[176].

Karttikeya also known as Murugan, Skanda, Kumara[177] and Subrahmanya, is the Hindu god of war[178]. He is the son of Parvati and Shiva, brother of Ganesha, and a god whose life story has many versions in Hinduism[179]. He is said to have power of curing diseases and protecting people from being possessed by evil spirits[180]. The *Nilmatapuran* refers to a special worship consisting of garlands, sandal, ornaments, food, *kukkuta*, etc. to be offered to him on the 6th day of the lunar Caitra with View to ensure the good health of the children[181]. Karttikeya worship in early Kashmir is borne out by the discovery of a fine six armed image of the generalissimo[182]. His temple at Pundravardhana is referred to by Kalhana[183].

Ganesa is the god of wisdom, intelligence, luck, and fortune. Prosperity and success will come wherever Ganesa is and He is the remover of obstacles. Ganesa who is today worshiped as one of the foremost deities of the Hindu pantheon, rose to prominence about the 6th century A.D. In the Purans he is generally described as the eldest son of Siva and the leader of his attendants. In many legends connected with his life, he is variously named as Vinayaka, Vakratunda, Ekadanta, Ganapati Vighnesvara, Akhuratha, Siddhidata, Heramba, Lambodara, Dividehaka, Gajanana and Bala-Ganapati[184]. He was considered as the bestower of Siddis. He is also described as the scribe of sage vyasa who dictated to him the famous epic Mahabharata[185]. A stone image of Ganesa along with an Ardhanarisvara image, have been found at Avantipura and may be dated of the 9th century A.D.[186]

Ganesa was especially worshiped on the fourth day of the bright half in the month of Magha with sweetmeats, incense, etc. according to the *Nilmatapurana* a special worship was offered to him Kashmir on the eighth day of the dark fortnight of the month of Jyestha and the day was called Vinayakastami[187]. In the town of Avantipur in Kashmir the cooked food, sweets, etc. were offered to him which were later on sold in the market[188]. Some images of Ganesa have also been discovered from the ruins of the city of Avantipura[189].

Agni occupies a very essential and sacred place in the Hindu religion. Agni, called Hutavaha and Hutasana and styled Bhagavata, is referred to in connection with funeral[190]. Agni is regarded as the friend and protector of humanity; in particular, he safeguards the home. Various forms of fire are associated with Agni and include the sun, the fire of the funeral pyre, and the digestive fire which is within all humans. *Nilmatapurana* revives ample evidences of Agni worship[191]. According to Kalhana the king Uccalas[192]father Malla[193] observed from his earliest time the cult of a sacred fire[194]. There was a shrine of fire Svayambhu at Suyam the present village of Nichhom[195].

Laksmi, is the Hindu goddess of wealth, fortune and prosperity[196] she is the wife and Shakti (energy) of Vishnu, one of the principal deities of Hinduism and the supreme Being in the Vaishnavism tradition[197]. King Pravarasena-ii[198] is credited with the establishment of five Shrines of the goddess Sri[199]. An image of Laksmi has been discovered from the historic town of Vijabror, modern Brar[200]. Another image found from the Avantisvami[201] temple at Avantipora. During the reign of Unmattavanti[202], a Brahman named Rakka, raised image of the goddess Sri under the appellation of Rakkajayadevi[203].

View to ensure the good health of the children[204]. Karttikeya worship in early Kashmir is borne out by the discovery of a fine six armed image of the generalissimo[205]. His temple at Pundravardhana is referred to by Kalhana[206].

REFERENCES

1. Fida. M. Hassnain, *Kashmir the Focus of Asiatic Civilization.*, p. 7.
2. Ved. Kumari., *The Nilamatapurana.*, 46-48.
3. P.N.K. Bamzai., *Cultural and Political History of Kashmir.*, Vol. I, p. 217.
4. Waters., on *Yuan Chwang*, i., p. 265.
5. F. Gladwin., *Ayeen Akbari* trns. p. 412.
6. W. Crooke, *Religion and folk lore of Northern India*, pp. 383-99.
7. S.C. Ray., *Early History and Culture of Kashmir.*, pp. 155-156.
8. R.T., I., 28, 29.
9. Ved.Kumari. *op.cit.*, p 187
10. *Ibid.*
11. *Ibid.*
12. R.T., I., 181.

13. R.T., I., 183. 184.
14. R.T. III., 490.
15. R.T., I. 222.
16. R.T., 1., 91
17. Fida. M. Hussain., *Buddhism in Kashmir.*, pp. 11-12.
18. *Ibid.*
19. Sarla Khosla., *Religious History of Buddhism in Kashmir.*, p.
20. Ved Kumara., *Nilmatapurana* v-i., p.
21. P.N.K. Bamzi., *Cultural and political History of Kashmir.*, p. 217.
22. Sarla Khosal *op.cit.*, p. 14.
23. S.C Ray, *Early History and Culture of Kashmir.*, p. 158.
24. Fida M hussain p. 12.
25. T. Waters., *Yaun Chwang's Travels in India*, Trans., Vol. I, p. 262.
26. R.T.I., 102.
27. S. Beal, *Buddhist records of the Western World.*, p. 150.
28. Thomas Waters, *op.cit.*, p. 261.
29. Fida m. Hussain., *Buddhism in Kashmir.*, p. 15.
30. S.L. Shali,., *Kashmir History and Archaeology through the Ages.*, p. 118.
31. S.C.Ray, *op.cit.*, p. 159.
32. R.T., I., 108.
33. R.T., I.,111, 112.
34. R.T., I. 112. 113
35. *Ibid.*
36. R.T., I., 131-146. *Kritva* met Jaloka and demanded human flesh. He offered his own. She compared him with Buddhisattvas who are free from five affictions and risk themselves to comfort others. On hearing this Jaloka revoked his orders and promised that,henceforth he will abstain from such acts.
37. D.D. Copleston., *Buddhism*, p. 371.
38. V. Trenckner, *Milindapanho*, p. 420.
39. Mrs. C.G, Bruce., *The Peep at Kashmir*, p. xvii.
40. R.T., I., 168.
41. R.T., I., 169,170.
42. Ibid.
43. Sarla Kshola., op.cit., p. 91.
44. Samuel Beal, *Buddhist records of the Western World.*, p. 117.
    P. Thomas, *Hindu Religion, Customs and Manners*, p. 53.
    H.C. Roychaudhuri., *Political History of Ancient India*, p. 475.

Hiuen Tsang has stated that the council was held in Kashmir, he had not only given the exact location but on the other hand Taranath ha mentioned 'Kundalwan' as a place where this great council was held (S. L. Shali, Kashmir history and archaeology through the ages, p 123.)

45. A. Kaul, *Buddhist Savantas of Kashmir*, p. 5.
46. J.N. Ganhar and P.N. ganhar, *Buddhism in Kashmir and Ladakh*. p. 33.
47. S.L. Shali, *op.cit.*, p. 123.
48. Obermiller., trans. *'History of Buddhism in India*, pp. 96-97.
49. Fida. M. Hussain, *op.cit.*, p. 21.
50. *Ibid.* p. 22
51. Mrs. C.G, Bruce., *op.cit.*, p. xvii.
52. R.T., I., 173.
53. H.H.,Wilson, *Hindu History of Kashmir*, p. 111.
54. R.T., I., 174
55. R.T., I 199, 200.
56. R.T., I. 289.
57. Panikkar, *Harsha of Kanuaj*, p. 2.
58. R.T., III. 2, 3, 4, 5.
59. R.T., III, 9.
60. R.T., III, 7.
61. R.T., III., 355.
62. R.T., iii 355.
63. R.T., IV., 7.
64. R.T., IV, 126.
65. R.T., IV., 188, 201-203.
66. R.T., iv., 200.
67. R.T., IV, 211.
68. R.T., IV, 216.
69. J.N. Ganhar and P.N. Ganhar., *op.cit.*, p. 105, Tantrism is usually regarded as belief in certain mantras (words or expressions possessing esopteri meaning) and meditational poses and practices for the attainment of the highest Truth. On a lower plane Tantrism is regarded as belief in magic and sorcery and certain secret rites and rituals for the attainment of various ends –good or bad.
70. Sarla khosla., *Ksemendra and his Times.*, p. 91.
71. R.T., IV., 402.
72. G.M.D. Sufi, *'Kasher', being a History of Kashmir*, p. 55.

73. R.C. Kak., *Ancient Monuments of Kashmir*, p. 161.
74. R.T. V., 2.
75. R.T., V., 66. Bhatta Kallata, is known as the pupil of Vasugupta who was the founder of Spandasastra branch of kashmirian Shaiva philosophy. The commentary written by him is called Spandasarvasva. It was written on his teachers work and is called Spandakarikas.
    N.K. Singh, *Buddhism in Kashmir*, pp. 129-30.
76. R.T., V., 64.
77. R.T., V., 128.
78. R.T., V., 161.
79. R.T., V., 262.
80. R.T., VI., 150-187.
81. R.T., VI., 171.
82. R.T., VI, 172, 173.
83. R.T., VI., 175.
84. R.T., VI., 176.
85. R.T. VI 77.
86. Sarla Khosla., *op.cit.*, p. 92.
87. A.M. Shastri., *India as seen in the Kuttani-Mata of Damodaragupta.*, p. 59.
88. R.T., I., 105. 106.
89. *Ibid.*
90. R.T*., I., 113.
    *R.T. = KALHAN'S RAJATRANGINI, Translated by M. A. STEIN.
91. R.T., I., 124.
92. R.T., I., 148.
93. R.T., I., 153.
94. R.T., I., 154.
95. R.T., I., 289.
96. R.T., I., 306
97. R.T., I., 312-316.
98. R.T., I., 329.
99. R.T., I 341.
100. R.T., I., 347
101. R.T., I., 348.
102. R.T., II., 14

103. R.T., III., 99.
104. R.T., III., 268-280.
105. R.T., III., 350.
106. R.T., III., 440- 263.
107. R.T., IV., 38.
108. R.T., IV., 190.
109. R.T., IV., 209.
110. R.T., IV. 214.
111. R.T., IV., 513.
112. R.T., V., 66.
113. R.T., V., 45-46.
114. R.T., V., 37-38.
115. R.T., V., 40.
116. R.T., V., 128.
117. R.T., V., 158.
118. R.T., VI., 137.
119. R. T., 172-173.
120. R.T., VII., 2.
121. R.T., VII., 115.
122. R., T., VII., 180.
123. R.T., VII., 185.
124. R.T., VII., 201.
125. R.T., VII., 525.
126. R.T., VII., 527.
127. R.T., VIII., 2409.
128. J.C. Chatterji, *Kashmir Shavism*, pp. 28-29.
129. *Ibid*. p. 32.
130. B.D. Chattopdhyaya, (ed.), *History of Science, Philosophy and Culture in Indian Civilization*, Vol. II, Part 5. (A Social History of Early India), p 188.
131. R.G. Bandarkar, *Vaishavism, Saivism, and Minor Religious Systems*, p. 186.
132. JC. Chatterji., *op.cit*., p. 34.
133. *Ibid*.
134. Ved, Kumari, *Nilamatapurana*, Vol. I, p. 139.
135. *Ibid*, pp. 140-141.
136. *Ibid*, p. 142.

137. R.T., III., 350, 351.
138. R.T., III. 144-158.
139. R.T., IV., 6.
140. R.T., IV., 4.
141. R.T., IV., 78.
142. R.T., IV., 80.
143. R.T., IV., 81.
144. R.T., IV., 183.
145. R.T., IV., 188.
146. R.T., IV., 193.
147. R.T., IV., 194, 195.
148. T.T., IV., 196.
149. R.T., IV., 197.
150. R.T., IV., 198.
151. R.T., IV., 275.
152. R.T., IV., 208.
153. R.T., IV., 209.
154. R.T., IV., 507-509.
155. R.T., IV., 659.
156. R.T., V., 45.
157. R.T., V., 23.
158. R.T., V., 25.
159. R.T., V., 28-29.
160. R.T., V., 99-100.
161. P.N.K. Bamzi, *op.cit.*, p. 223.
162. R.T., V., 224.
163. R.T., V., 245.
164. S.C. Ray, *Early History and Culture of Kashmir*, p. 180.
165. Kamla Chauhan., *Cultural History Of Northern India.*, p. 176.
166. Ved Kumari., *Nilamataourana* p. 165.
167. A.M. Shastri, *India as seen in the Kuttani- Mata of Damodaragypta*, p. 76.
168. *Ibid.*
169. R.T., III., 386.
170. R.T., III., 462.
171. R.T., iv 126-371.
172. R.T., iv 192.
173. R.T., V 22.

174. R.T., v 449.
175. R.T., vii 696-709.
176. R.T.
177. James G Lochtefeld, *The illustrated Encyclopedis of Hinduism*, p. 377.
178. *Ibid.* pp. 655-656.
179. Constance Jones and James D. Rayan, *Encyclopedia of Hinduism*, p. 228.
180. Kamla Chauhan, *op.cit.*, p. 177.
181 Ved Kumara, *Nilmatapurana.*, p. 166.
182. R.C. KAK., Handbook, p. 66.
183. R., T., iv. 422
184. Allice Getty, *Ganesa*, pxxv.
185. *Ibid.* p. 234.
186. S.C. Ray, *op.cit.*, p. 182.
187. Ved Kumara., *op.cit.*, pp 165-66.
188. B.N. Sharma., *Social Life In Northern India.*, p. 161.
189. *Ibid.*
190. A.M. Shastri., *op.cit.*, p. 77.
191. Ved kumara., *op.cit.*, p. 169.
192. R.T., vii. 1183.
193. *ibid.*
194. R.T., *op. cit.*, vii 1474.
195. *Ibid.* I 34.
196. James G Lochtefeld., *op.cit.* pp. 385-386.
197. Anand Rao, *Soteriologies of India*, p 167.
198. M.A. Stain *op.cit*, iii., 109.
199. *Ibid.* iii. 353
200. R.C. Kak, *op.cit*, p. 58.
201. R.T., v 45.
202. R.T., v 414.
203. R.T., v 426.
204. Ved Kumara, *Nilmatapurana.*, p. 166.
205. R.C. KAK., Handbook, p. 66.
206. R.,T., iv. 422.

7

Dress, Ornaments and Cosmetics

One of the important aspects of the social life is the dress of the people. Contemporary literature, sculptures and the accounts of foreign travellers enable one to form a general idea of the various modes of clothing and costumes popular with the masses, the wealthy and nobility of the times.

The literature of the period refers to various kinds of clothes worn according to season. The *Amarakosa* mentions the three main kinds i.e. cotton, silk and woollen garments. The cotton cloth had four varieties made of *Valkam* (bark of tree), *Chhaum* (linseed fibre), *Bhanga* (hemp cloth) and *Karpsam*(cotton plant)[1]. The silk clothes also were of three varieties known as *vathram*, *Kauseya*, and *Krimikosoth*. The woollen clothes were made of hair or wool of animals skin (*Mrigromjam*). Chinese silk was a very costly textile. The gift of a pair of garments made from china silk was sufficient to lure a courtesan[2]. China silk enjoyed great popularity in ancient India at least from the Maurya period, and from that time onward we have a continuous chain of references to it in Sanskrit and Prakrit literature[3].

In Kashmir, while the climate conditions obliged the people to wear mostly woollen clothes. During cold season woollen garments of various kinds were used. Kalhana mentions that during the winter, people used to wear heavy or woollen garments[4].

We have both literary and archaeological evidence as regards the dress and ornaments of early inhabitants of

Kashmir. R.C. Kak believed that there was marked influence of central Asian dress upon Kashmir since Kushanas. We can study about this dress with the help of sculptures and terracotta figures.[5] One of the brick tiles of *Harvan*, for instance depicts a lady wearing a transparent robe, a close fitting turban and larger earrings. Another tile shows a female dancer wearing loose robes and trousers. While a third one had a figure of a female musician dressed in fitting trousers and *Turkman* caps."[6]

However changes took place with the growth of contact with Indian plains during the Karkota rule. A long robe hanging down the shoulders to the knees, tied up at the waist with a girdle or belt formed the dress of men folk. This cloth still exists in the shape of *Phiran*.

Male Dress

Men wore a variety of garments. The rich wore cloths fashioned from costly textiles like china silk and *patika*. Their clothes were sometimes interwoven with threads of gold. Coloured garments were very much in favour. We have references to the son of an influential government officer attired in garments dyed with saffron and worked with golden threads. The poor dressed themselves in old tattered garments[7], sometimes made by joining many a piece together. Their cloths were made from a rough variety of cotton textiles[8]. Apart from regional variations, the rich, the middle classes, the poor and the destitute had their own way of putting on their dresses. For example, the royal personage put on robes that fell up to the earth[9].

The head dress has been frequently mentioned in Sanskrit literature as Usnisa. Sometimes common people used to wear ordinary *Sirahsata* to cover their head[10]. Turban is rarely seen used by the common people in the sculptures of this age, though it was held in considerable esteem. We have a reference in *Kuttanimatam*, where a prince has been described wearing a kind of head dress. It seems that it was a square or rectangular cloth, which was tied round head[11]. The dress of a male consisted of an angarakha and a turban with many folds. The turban was sometimes dyed with turmeric[12].

The costume of men usually consisted of two garments of long pieces of clothes. Literary evidence suggests the use of stitched upper garments like *angarakshaka, kurpasaka,* etc. the *angarakshaka* was probably like the *angarkha* of later times or a loose and long coat almost like a *kurta* of our days. The long loose robe or cloak, covering the body from shoulders to knee continued to be worn by the masses even today, both men and women. While the masses also covered their shoulders with a thick and coarse blanket (*sthulakambala*) the rich used a fine one (*kutta*). Latter called shawls, the fine blankets used by well to do women were sometimes made of the goat hair, emanating the fragrance of musk. Bilhana calls them pattika Rankavanam[13].

The great Chinese pilgrim Hiuen Tsang who reached the valley from Urusha(Hazara) in the west in 631, writes that the climate of Kashmir was cold and stem. There is much snow but little wind. The people wear leather doublets and clothes of white linen[14]. The low temperature of the valley, particularly at the time of winter, must have compelled the people to employ woollen garments to cover their body. During cold season woollen garments of various kinds were used. Kalhana mentions that during the winter, people used to wear heavy or woollen garments[15]. The woollen kambala was known as Rallak Kambala[16]. Kambala is woollen blanket and pravarana referred to in connection with festival of the new snow fall, seems to be the same as pravara mentioned in the *Mahabharata* as a cloth offering protection against cold[17]. Brahmacarins wore girdles (mekhalika) which when broken, were replaced. Katitra or waist- band was also an important item of dress. Dhoti continued to be the most popular garment worn by men. Men used to wear long and short Dhoti.

Men, rich and poor alike, used shoes, Kalhana refers in his *Rajatrangini* to leather shoes[18]. Shoes were a necessary luxury; but the poor could ill-afford to change them very now and then, and as such they continued to use them until they became completely unserviceable. The rich on the other hand used luxurious shoes. Besides leather shoes Ksemandra mentions peacock shoe (Mayuropanat) which was a fashion during his times. They also use wooden sandals (Khrew). King Chakravarman's court was, "made resplendent by the white head-dresses."[19] We have references in *Kuttanimatam* the shoes had still mode soles, important from central Asia and with bees-wax placed inside for a soothing touch[20]. They were also fond of using shoes producing noise as the wearer moved[21].

Female Dress

The women wore upper garment and lower garment ordinarily both these garments appear to have been unstitched the lower one being like present day dhoti and upper one being used in the fashion of the uttariya or scarf[22]. According to Ksemendra no stitched dress were worn by women. Only ancala which seems to be a loose cloth was used[23]. Kalhana refers to the transparent garments worn during summer. Sulaiman an Arab traveller who visited India during the 10th century A.D. appreciates the then clothes produced in the country in the following words, 'there is stuff made in this country which is not to be found elsewhere, so fine and delicate is this material that a dress made of it may be passed through a signet ring, it is made of cotton and we have seen it[24]. Fashionable ladies loved to wear soft, clean and perfumed cloths. They were very fond of Chinese silk[25]. They used silk their ansuka from china which was again a loose cloth[26]. Like men, women were also fond of using coloured cloths. Garments dyed with saffron commanded special favour. Even the elderly women had a preference for clean white cloths[27].

Dupatta appears to have been an important item of dress worn by ladies just to add beauty and grace. There are frequent references of dupatta worn by ladies. Prostitutes are stated to have used white dupattas[28].

Side by side with unstitched cloths, stitched garments were also in vogue. Ksemendra mentions two such items of dress viz, Kancuka and Varabana. Both these cloths appear to have been very much similar to one another as served the same purpose[29]. Kanchuka was a sort of very short jacket sufficient just to corner the breasts and was worn with the help of bands. Kalhana referred the same garment as "kanchuka"[30], Kalhana explains it as, "the brassiere which traced the curves of the breast a concealed the upper half of the arms". It seems to have been a very common garment as we find that it has been frequently represented in female sculptures of the period. The varabana is said to have been worn on the breasts and put off at the time of sexual intercourse. If intervened between the bosoms and necklace. It may be noted in this connection that many Sanskrit writers regard these words as synonymous.

The commonest form of a lower garment amongst the women folk was sari. It was worn in different styles during the period under review. Sometimes the ladies used to wear the dress which was called Nivi. In Kashmir the dress of women was mainly composed of probably a sari and jacket. During the reign of Harsha the ladies wore a long lower garment, the tail end of which touches floor[31]. They wore the lower garment by putting a knot (nivi) to it[32].

Reference to pair of clothes worn by Vishnu a pair of clothes (one shining like the lightning and the other china silk resembling the rays of the moon) worn by Nila, a pair of clothes to be offered to a Brahman and a pair of cloths to be given in charity on Atyantamahati indicates that the male as well as the female dress in Kashmir comprised of two garments the upper and the lower one[33]. Mention is made of white and coloured clothes. In *Samayamatrka*, Kalavati (prostitute) wears most coloured dress, valuable jewellery and lovely hair etc to attract the customers[34]. The term "ahata" is used for new cloths[35].

Dress of the Soldiers

Soldiers always constitute a class by themselves in the society. Their dress includes head covering, an upper garment and the lower garment. Turban was the most popular head dress of soldiers. Sometimes these soldiers wore rectangular or square cloth to cover the head[36]. Sometimes they wore metal hat made of iron. Sometimes they decorated their heads with flowers or pearls[37]. These references indicate that probably such soldiers belonged to the higher or officer class. The Military officers used to wear coat, covering the chest and extending up to the middle of the thighs. In *Rajatrangini* we read of soldiers wearing a short coat of bright colour and named it as "Ardhoruka"[38]. Soldiers used to wear different types of lower garments e.g., trousers and dhoti. Bilhana and Kalhana both mentions that the end of the garment dangled at the back and touched the ground, because they were worn quite loosely by the warriors[39]. In order to keep the dhoti securely in place it seems that another piece of cloth was used as a belt called "Mekhala". It was tied round the waist over the upper edges of dhoti with a knot. In the battle field, leather strap was used for guarding loins[40]. These leather or wood straps were known as ' Kavach' they have been referred frequently in the literature[41]. Kalhana also describes Virapatta as a favourite dress of thieves[42]. Dr. S.C. Ray, refers to a terracotta figure in which the armed horseman is dressed in the said dress[43].

R.C. Ray, points out that long hairs to which comb were attached was also in fashion.[44] Sometimes, tassels of varied colours were joined with the hair. Kings and nobles also braided their hairs in various styles. Ksemandra speaks of a man whose hair is artificially curled and who also used beard-netting (Smasruvestana). Keeping beard was popular among both young and old men and king Sussala was nick named Lamba-kurca, meaning long bearded.[45]

Ornaments

The decorative value of ornaments has been recognised in all climes and at all times, and Kashmir has been no exception to this rule. The age under review is particularly rich in the types and designs of ornaments noticed particularly in the sculptures of the period. Considerably information about those in fashion during that age is also available from literary and epigraphic sources[46]. The passion for adornment was much stronger in Kashmir than in any other of ancient India. The literature and sculpture of the period reveal that the "clothes were simple and few ornaments were complex and many. There is at times so much variety even about types that it becomes difficult to be sure about the various minute differences that characterised the. The ornaments were worn by both sexes. Our literature abounds in the descriptions of ornaments worn by both the sexes. There is no part of body for which an appropriate ornament was not designed. The rich and poor were alike crazy for adornments and satiated their cravings in accordance with their respective means.

The available sources reveal that the women were fond of decorating their hair with ornaments known as Lalatika. Lalatika was an ornament worn on the forehead from one ear to another along with pendant in the middle. It was very similar to modern Vendi or Mangtika. It seems to have been very popular in Kashmir[47]. The ladies decorated their hair with strings of small beads or pearls in different styles. Sometimes the hair bun was decorated with pearl strings. The women of Kashmir were also fond of decorating the end of their braid or locks with twined golden string[48]. It is also possible that ornaments like Kanakapatta, Lalatapatta etc. were also worn in to decorate the forehead[49].

The ear ornaments were worn by both the sexes. According to Kalhana's, evidence too the male population of Kashmir used ornaments. These consisted chiefly of finger-rings, ear-rings, necklaces and bracelets[50]. The most popular ear ornament worn by men and women of all ranks was the 'kanaka-tadi'. Probably this very ornament is referred to under the name "tadi-yuga (a pair of tadis) by the Kashmiri poet Ksemendra,[51] showing there by that it continued to enjoy popularity in Kashmir in the eleventh century A.D. The women of Kashmir also had liking for wearing "kanakpatra" or gold leaf. It was also known as "kanakanadi"[52]. The ear ornaments made of worry were known as dantapatra and pankti[53]. These were generally called karnabhushanas or ornaments of the ear. Some other peculiar ornaments known as Sisaptraka and Dalabitaka are known from literature and it is interesting to note, that there was also a fashion of putting on different types of ornaments in each ear[54]. Besides the common ear ring (kundala) three other ornaments were worn by men on the ears viz, dalavitaka, sisa patra and danta pankti[55]. In *Kuttanimata* Damodaragupta describes the son of an officer in king's service who wears rings one of which is called Dalabitaka and other Sisapatraka[56].

From the available sources it appears that the women of Kashmir wore an ear ornament which was known as, "Dij-hor" or egg shaped solid but intricately engraved two piece set, hanging from both the ears; it consisted of a strong thread (atahor) the end of which was covered with a hollow ornaments in various designs. In Srinagar museum a sculpture (of 10th century) depicting the bird of the Buddha both Mayadevi and other lady are wearing 'dezi-hor" just as it is worn today by married women of Kashmir[57]. Kalhana tells us that it was king Harsha who broke age old customs which restricted wearing of earrings and turban to kings only. He however desired his officers to dress themselves befitting their rank.[58] Cunningham also noted about Harsha's interest for south Indian fashions.[59]

The literature and sculpture of the period reveal that a variety of necklaces were worn by all classes of men and women during the period under study. Necklaces (Hara) worn by the male and female were prepared of gold and precious stones (pearls and blue stones) reaching down to the chest. Damodaragupta takes great delight in describing the Necklace, hara, haralata, as enjoying the company of the heavy bosoms[60]. These necklaces usually consisted of one or more pearls. Damodaragupta records the dress of an attendant who has got in his neck coarse and cheap kacavartakamala and conch shell in his hand[61]. The costly necklaces were generally worn by the people of high rank, while on the other hand people of lower strata of the society satisfied their desire of self adornment by wearing necklaces made of cowries (shells), cheap glass, beads, lac, and sting of Gunja fruits[62].

The armlets were also worn by both the sexes, and were made in various designs. Sometimes the designs were very complicated and were stud with pearl or precious stones. Damodaragupta mentions that a wealthy man is said to wear necklace, armlet and wristlet made of golden and coral beads[63].

A special variety of armlet known as "valaya kalapi" was very much liked by the women of Kashmir. This kind of armlet had the "face of a peacock" and "moon shaped end"[64].

The ornaments worn on the wrist was commonly known as valaya and kataka. The number of bracelets to be worn on a wrist was not fixed. A number of valayas was sometimes put on each wrist[65]. The sculpture of the period also reveals numerous examples, which confirm that women of Kashmir had great liking for wearing rows of bangles. Sometimes men also used to wear bangles of couch shell[66].

Cosmetics

Ever since stepping into the age of civilization mankind has paid considerable attention to physical adornment. The people in Kashmir too have been in practice of using items of cosmetics. Both men and women made an extensive use of cosmetics and perfumes to enhance their bodily charm. Before adorning the body both men and women used to take a bath with several kinds of anguents. The people of Kashmir were quite familiar with a large variety of pastes powders prepared with sandal wood, camphor, and jarina of flowers etc. the literary records of the period frequently mention that men and women used to decorate their faces with powder, paste and many scented articles just as in modern times[67]. After drying, parting and plaiting the hair, married ladies applied, Sindura in the middle of forehead[68]. Tilaka seems to have been commonly applied by both men and women, in different styles. Generally the Tilaka was made with musk, saffron, and sometimes with white sandal[69]. The use of pastes made up of leaves and mustard, seeds is also attested by Damodaragupta[70]. Ladies applied Sindura signifying their married status. Literature however attests to the use of tilakas even by unmarried ladies. Candana was used for tilaka by dark complexioned women[71]. *Narmamal* mentions candana tilaka in common use. Fair complexioned women used kasturi tilak[72]. The married women decorate their forehead with painted marks[73].

As face is regarded to be the most important part of the body, people took great interest in decorating their faces to make it more beautiful and charming. Mention may be made of the different ways in which facial beauty was sought to be enhanced. We often read in the literature that women used to rub their checks with musk and saffron paste to make the complexion of the face whiter[74]. The epigraphic records also testify the fact that women were in habit of decorating their check with various designs, with sandal and saffron. Besides the cheeks, the lips were also coloured to make the face attractive. The women used to colour their lips with laksras (lac dye)[75]. The sculptures of the period also testify to the fact that the women of the period used lipstick. Wax was also applied on the lips to keep them soft during the winter season. They used betal (betal-eating) for reddening the lips[76]. The next important item of face decoration was the makeup of the eyes. From the frequent references in the literature we learn that the eyes were adorned with kajala or collirium to blacken the eyes[77].

Large scale use of leaves and flowers was atypical feature of ancient Indian toilette. The use of flowers as ornaments is well attested by literature. Flowers were used as ornaments and fashioned into various types of garlands. Flower garlands were worn by both men and women. It appears that flowers were chosen with an eye on the season and their colour etc, to match with the dress. The flowers were generally used for decoration of hair and also in ears. Garland of colourful flowers were decorated on the loosed braid, and bun. The garland used for decorating the hair was known as Garbhaka. Reference is made to various sorts of scents, perfumes, unguents, flowers and garlands[78].

REFERENCES

1. R.T*., VII, 295-300
   *Kalhana's Rajatrangini, translated by M. A. Stein.
2. A.M. Shastri., *Kuttani-mata of Damodragupta*, p. 133.
3. J.C. Jain, *Life in Ancient India as depicted in the Jain canon*, p. 129.
4. R.T., V., 196.
5. R.C. Kak, *Ancient Monuments of Kashmir*, New Delhi, 1987, p. 50.
6. P.N.K.Bamzai, *op.cit.*, p. 262.
7. J.C. Jain, *op.cit.*, p. 407.
8. *Ibid.*
9. R.T., VII., 930.
10. A.M.Shastri., *op.cit*, v 356
11. Dr. Kamla Chauhan., *Cultural History of Northern India.*, p. 55.
12. Sarla Khosla., *Ksemendra and his Times.*, p. 148.
13. M.L. Kapur., *Kingdom of Kashmir.*, p. 253.
14. S. Beal., Buddhist Records of Western World, p. 148.
15. R.T., V 196.
16. *Ibid.*
17. Ved Kumari. *Nilamatapurana.*, p. 116.
18. R.T., VIII. 137.
19. P.N.K. Bamzai, *op.cit.*, p. 263.
20. A.M. Shastri., *op.cit.*, p. 135.
21. *Ibid.*
22. A.M. Shastri., *op.cit.*, 135.
23. Sarala. Khosla., *op.cit.*, p. 148.
24. R.T., V., 196.
25. A.M. Shastri. *op.cit.*, 135.
26. Sarla. Khosla., *op.cit.*, p. 148.
27. *Ibid.*
28. Kamla Chauhan. *op.cit.*, p. 51.
29. A.M. Shastri. *op.cit.*, p. 136.
30. R.T., VII., 930.
31. R.T., VII., 930.
32. A. M.Shastri, *op.cit.*, p. 135.
33. Ved Kumari, *op.cit.*, pp. 116, 117.
34. Sarla Khosla, *op.cit.*, p. 148.

35. Ved Kumari, *op.cit.*, p. 117.
36. R.T., VII., 1893.
37. R.T., VIII, 280-85.
38. R.T., VII., 923-24.
39. R.T., VIII., 1735..
40. *Ibid.*
41. R.T., VIII., 283.
42. R.T., V., 333-VIII. 1774.
43. S.C. Ray, *op.cit.*, p. 210.
44. *Ibid.* p. 283.
45. M.L.Kapur, *Kingdom of Kashmir*, Srinagar, 2005, p. 255.
46. R.T., VIII., 2883.
47. R.T., VII., 928-931.
48. R.T., VII., 928-931.
49. *Ibid.*
50. R.T., VIII., 241, IV, VII, 349-352, VI, 749, 812, 876-878, 922, VIII, 329, 1744.
51. A.M. Shastri., *op.cit.*, p. 1143.
52. Jagan Nath Pathak, *Kuttanimatam Kavyam*, p. 358.
53. *Ibid.* p. 62.
54. *Ibid.*
55. A.M. Shastri., *op.cit.*, p. 139.
56. Jagan Nath Pathak, *op.cit.*, pp. 63-65.
57. P.N. Bazaz., *Daughters of Vitasta*, p. 8, The ornament gained sanctity and was considered as important sigh of subhag (Married bless)
58. S.K. Saxsana, *Political History of Kashmir*, New Delhi, 1974, p. 204.
59. Cunningham, *coins of Medieval India from Seventh century Down to the Muhammedan conquests*, Varansi, 1967, p. 34.
60. A.M. Shastri., *op.cit.*, p. 142.
61. Jagan Nath Pathak, *op.cit.*, p. 67.
62. *Ibid.*
63. *Ibid.* 739-742.
64. *Ibid.* 343
65. A.M. Shastri., *op.cit.*, p. 141.
66. Jagan Nath Pathak, *op.cit.*, 67.
67. Jagan Nath Pathak, *op.cit.*, 607-758.
68. *Ibid.* 62.

69. *Ibid.* 597.
70. *Ibid.* 740.
71. Sarla Khosla., *op.cit.*, p. 149.
72. *Ibid.*
73. R.T., IV., 130.
74. S.C. Ray, *op.cit.*, 256.
75. R.T., III., 415.
76. Sarla Khosla, *op, cit.*, p 149.
77. R.T., I., 207-209.
78. Ved Kumari, *op.cit.*, p. 117.

8

Food and Drinks

Considerable care and attention was paid by the people to food and drink during the period under review. In fact food was supposed to be an important factor and had, from the beginning, been regarded as the governing factor of human longevity.[1]

For the sake of convenience, the eating habits of the people may be dealt with in two broad group's viz., the vegetarians and non vegetarians and account for their habits regarding their food and drink. This division too is qualified by regional peculiarities which are mostly governed by the agricultural produce, climatic conditions and other factors involved in it. For example, the people inhabiting the mountainous terrains of the North-west, Kashmir and the Punjab differed widely in their food habits from those living in the lower delta of the Ganga or Bengal and Eastern-Bihar[2]

The art of cooking attained a high degree of perfection in ancient Kashmir. It was considered to be one of the most important and appreciable art cultivated by women in ancient times. Women used to acquire efficiency in the art and learnt how to cook innumerable variety of food, which were eaten by chewing, licking and drinking.

From the very Ancient times in Kashmir rice was the staple food. Damodaragupta refers to three different varieties of paddy, viz., *Sali*[3], Kalama[4] and *Anu*. '*Danya* (rice crop) and *Sali* have often been mentioned in the early literature of the valley. The scarcity of this commodity invariably resulted in famine.[5] The *Nilmatpurana* and *Narmamala* (by Kshemandra) speak of the various preparations made from rice for example, boiled rice, cakes of rice or barley mixed with ghee, flattened rice, the eating of which was prohibited in the day time, and milk porridge of rice mixed with purified butter.[6] They prepared Apupas modern Kulcha out of rice and barley mixture. Adding honey to this flour, it was given the shape of a round cake and then baked in Clarified butter on slow fire.

Pulses too were in use during this time. Damodaragupta in his *Kuttamitakavya* speaks of three kinds of pulses, *Kulattha*[7] (*Dolichos uniflorus*) *Cana* (horse gram) and *Masura* (*Ervum hirstum*).[8] Kshemandra mentions a fourth Varity called *Mudga*[9]. According to Damodaragupta beggars and ordinary travelers, who received these different sorts of rice and pulses as alms from different houses had to eat them mixed up together[10]. Mudga seems to have been more popular for the convalescents as it is easily digested.[11] Gram was used for the preparation of both vegetarian and non vegetarian dishes. The literature of the period reveals that *urad* (pulse), *munga* (green grain) and Pease were used as pulse, and in the preparation of many other dishes. Kulth, chana, and masura were popular pulses in Kashmir in the Gangetic valley and in Gujarat[12].

Milk was also one of the principle items of diet, literature of the period reveals that peasants and herdsmen supplied milk, butter, ghee to the people, and it was consumed in various forms. Ksemendra mentions milk and milk items include milk, *ksira* i.e., *kheera* (made of milk and rice), curds, and lassi (curd and water)[13]. Many sweet dishes were prepared from milk like *Ksirprakara*, *Ksirvata* and *Ksirayastika*. Ghee, milk, garlic, onion were considered as energy giving[14].Barley was poor man's food. "Sesames (*tila*) were especially taken on certain special days, such as the festival of *Tiladevadasi*."[15]

A large variety of Vegetables also were widely grown and taken, and they find mention in the literature of the period. The use of garlic and onions seem to have been favored in the western parts of the country, particularly in Kashmir[16].

It was supposed to be an expression of honor if onion was presented to the teachers or to the elders though this practice did not find favor elsewhere in the country[17]. Amongst vegetables the bottle gourd, cucumber, radish, brinjal, various types of beans, carrots, etc., were commonly used. Mustered stalks were generally taken during winter. Some fruits, leaves, roots and legumes of many plants were also used as vegetables[18]. *Rajtarangini* mentioned a kind of wild growing herb of bitter taste called *Utpalasaka,* which was generally taken by the common people. The herb, now known as *Upalhak,* grows abundantly on the mountain slopes of Kashmir and forms one of the commonest vegetable of the Kashmir cuisine.[19]

Though, India is generally believed to have led the world in vegetarianism since very early times, the evidence of literature, epigraphs and sculptures of the period points to non-vegetarianism as well. Among the non-vegetables, mutton was freely taken by people as Kashmir falls in the cold Himalayan region; the fact that the *Nilmatpurana* found it necessary to proscribe meat eating on the days dedicated to Vishnu's worship indicates the popularity of animal food in ancient Kashmir[20]. In the 13th century A.D. Marco Polo found that flesh with rice and other food grains formed the principal food of the Kashmiri's[21]. Animals like sheep, goat, fish, water and land birds like sparrow, doves and other animals were killed and allowed to be taken for food. In the cold season people relished eating pork with newly husked rice. Fragrant and tasteful curry of bird and goat meat was very much liked. The literature of the period mentions various kinds of preparations of meat. Meat of fowls and rams was also eaten[22]. Various edible birds too were massacred.[23] According to Kalhana, domestic pigs were eaten in Kashmir without any adverse notice[24]. People of valley besides all these diets; eat fried meat with high spices. Ksemendra in his works mentions many a times about meat eaters and meat. He writes that the meat of a lamb or a he goat was taken by the students[25]

Consumption of meat juice (*mamsa rasa*) is said to cure bodily pain. Prostitutes consumed meat soup for removing the body ache caused by wanton sexual intercourse with men. Ksemenrda in his *Deopadesa* also states that a prostitute regains youth by consuming fish juice, ghee, milk and onions. Kalhana also mentions fish-broth as an aphrodisiac[26].

Of the animals whose flesh was consumed particular reference is made to the fish. It was largely consumed in Kashmir[27]. Damodragupta describes the manner of catching, cooking and eating the fish. A snare stained with fish was thrown into the water; when the fish was thus caught, it was cooked with spice; after eating the flesh, its skin and bones were thrown away[28]. Fish-juice (*Matseyayusa*) was considered to be a particularly strength giving tonic food. The Gauda student of *matha* cooks the fish himself and eats after keeping fast for the whole day. This soup was perhaps prepared with fish and onion and was a favorite in Kashmir[29].

It should, however, be noted that regional considerations were also responsible for non-vegetarianism to a great extent among the masses dwelling in different parts of the country. People inhabiting the regions watered by the lower Ganga were in the habit of eating fish; those in the North West and Kashmir had to depend on meat in the absence of pulses and lack of other staple cereals[30].

For the preparation of good food, spices and condiments were used. The literature of our period supply information about the various spices that were used in the diet. The merchants trading in salt, pepper, ginger and vegetables which were collectively *Kirana*. Thus it is clear that spices were mixed, up to make food more tasteful and they were used along with ghee and oil for preparation of vegetables, fish and meat.[31] Black pepper, ginger, salt, *jayaphala* and *catika*(*cataru*) were used[32]. Oil formed a staple article for food.

As in rest of India, so in Kashmir has been from the ancient times famous for its different varieties of fruits. Kalhan even goes to the extent of saying that the grapes, which are scare even in heaven, were common in Kashmir.[33] The

Nilmatapurana also refers to it.[34] In the ancient times grapes were found in plenty in *Martand* but was later restricted to areas around the Dal shores. Besides, grapes, pomegranate was another fruit which was common in the valley. Fruits which are famous nowadays like apple, Pears, walnuts, straw berries may have been an ancient history because in the texts names of the different fruits are rarely mentioned, and was lavishly consumed by the people. There are several references in *Rajtarangini* to people men and women, who were addicted to drink.[35] The popularity of wine in Kashmir is evident from the fact that on certain religious festivals like the new snowfall Day, the second Mahimana and the Iramanjari-pujana the drinking of wine is recommended in the *Nilmata puran*[36]. Though drinking wine has been condemned by our ancient law givers, we have innumerable examples, which prove that wine was very popular, and it was enjoyed equally by members of both the sexes and of all ranks. In spite of sastrik injunctions forbidding the Brahmanas from taking wine, we notice that the Brahamans had been taking to drinking during the period under review. In the *Kuttanimatam* we read of Brahamana youth wasting their time in drinking (in the company of dancing girls)[37]. In *Kalavilasa* Ksemendra narrates many types of intoxications, passions, betel, wine, women, gambling, hunting and drinking[38]. In *Narmamala* in the yajna performed by kayastha, guru takes food and wine with his followers. He drinks so much that loosing self-control, dances along with all intoxicated men and women[39].'Juices from grape and sugarcane, both of which grew in the valley, were distilled into spirituous liquors.'[40] A cold, sweet drink (Tuhina Sarkaran), mentioned by Kalhana, which was taken with great delight in hot summer days.

Prostitutes were particularly addicted to drinking which imparted fragrance and a coppery complexion to the face. Men were very anxious to partake of the wine offered by their beloved after she had tasted it[41].

Ksemendra mentions wine and meat and pitchers full of wine from which wine could be taken again and again. Taking wine to the point of loosing self-control is also alluded to. Divara intoxicated danced naked, and the broken wine pitchers lay by his side. Wine mixed with *kasturi* (more intoxicating) was also taken. Wine was prepared from grapes[42].

It may be noted that people were generally in the habit of taking betel-leaves along with the customary ingredients of lime, catechu and areca-nuts. This was supposed to help in digesting food and at the same time strengthening the gums and the teeth. Alberuni noted that the teeth of the people were generally colored because of their habit of chewing betel-leaves[43]. The *Rajatrangini* refers to a betel-leaf dealer who became an intimate of a king of Kashmir because of his supplying these to his court from far-off regions[44]. It seems to be imported from outside. As betal- leaves were supplied to king Ananta by a merchant who imported them[45].

REFERENCES

1. R.C. Majumdar, *The Age of Imperial Unity*, pp. 554-55
2. These peculiarities are to be noted even in the *Mahabharata*. Perhaps it was with an eye on regional considerations that the later commentators particularly Vijnanesvara and Bhavadeva Bhatta made certain concessions in food habits of the people. T.N. Pandey., *Journal of the U.P. Historical Society*, Vol. XIV, p. 140.
3. It corresponds to the transplanted variety now called *jadahan*.
4. According to Monier Williams (*Sanskrit_ English Dictionary*), it is now sown in May or June and harvested in December or January.
5. P.N.K. Bamzai, *Political and Cultural History of Kashmir*,Vol. I p. 261.
6. M.L. Kapur, *Kingdom of Kashmir*, p. 249.
7. Now called *kulathi*.
8. A.M. Shastri, *India as seen in the kuttani-mata of damodaragupta*, p. 131.
9. R.C.Ray, *Early History and Culture of Kashmir.*, p. 280.
10. A.M Shastri *op.cit*, p. 131.
11. Y.B. Singh., *Social Life in Ancient India*, p. 104
12. Dr. Kamala Chauhan, *Cultural History of Northern India.*, p. 85.
13. Sarla Khosla, *Ksemendra and his Times.*, p. 154.
14. *Ibid*.
15. M.L. Kapir, *Kingdom of Kashmir*, Srinagar, 2005, p. 249.

16. R T*., vii, 522
 *R.T- Kalhana's Rajatrangini, Translated by M.A. Stein
17. *Ibid.*143.
18. Sarla Khosla, *op.cit.*, p 154.
19. S.C. Ray, *op.cit.*, pp. 249-50.
20. Ved kumara, *Nilmatapurana*, p. 119.
21. Henry Yule, *Travels of Marco Polo*, p. 166.
22. M. Kaul., *Narmala of Ksemendra* p. 124.
23. *Ibid.* pp. 249-50.
24. R.T., v, 119; vii, 1149.
25. Sarla Khosala *op.cit* p. 155.
26. R.T., vii. 522.
27. R.T., v. 119.
28. A.M. Shastri *op.cit.*, p.132.
29. Sarla Kosha *op.cit.*, p. 155.
30. R.C. Majumdar, *History of Bengal*, pp. 611-12.
31. Sarla Kosha *op.cit.*, p. 154.
32. *Ibid.*
33. *Gazetteer of Kashmir and Ladakh* (complied under the direction of quarter master general in India in Intelligence branch, Vivek Publication, Delhi, 1974), p. 8.
34. R.T., Vol. I P. 42.
35. P.N.K. Bamzai, *op.cit.*, p. 262.
36. Ved kumara *Nilmatapurana* p. 83.
37. Dr. kamala chauhan, *op.cit.*, p. 88.
38. Sarla Kosha *op.cit.*, p. 156.
39. *Ibid.*
40. S.C.Ray, *op.cit.*, p. 282.
41. A.M. Shastri, *op.cit.*, p. 132.
42. Sarla Kosha *op.cit.*, p. 156.
43. E.C. Sachau., *Alberuni's India*, p 180.
44. R.T., VII, 190-93.
45. *Ibid.*

9

Conclusion

Kashmir is known as the paradise on earth. It has been acclaimed as a land of bliss, peace and contentment. Kashmir has been described as the largest valley mountains in the world. Kashmir has everything that can stimulate a creative mind and a compelling passion. There is a lot of variety in which there is something for everybody's interest. It has scenic beauty for artists, high mountains for mountaineers, and other adventure and places suited for specialized sports and everything that can stimulate the creative genius and the art. Kashmir has remained the home of learning and creative art and literature, from ancient times it has contributed to the growth of philosophy, sciences, language, literature and discourses in religion.

The peculiar heritage of the life of its people has, however, to be understood not only in terms of their antiquity, but also in terms of an amalgam of different ethics, religious and cultural influences working on them through the slow process of time. The persistence of tribal survivals and their influence on the Kashmiri social structure, and the interaction of complex historical forces from the time of the Mon-Khmer group of people. The Nagas and the Aryans down to the Mughal invasions have thus largely contributed to the making of the Kashmiri society. What the country presents is, therefore a composite entity that has received and absorbed cultures, creeds and people of many races down the ages.

Yet another significant fact which strikes most about Kashmir is that the various influences which have affected the life of its people from time to time have flowed mostly from the side of India. Whether it was the language or religion, dress or diet, art or architecture, any change in these spheres in India had its vibrations in Kashmir also. And there appear nothing surprising about this. But they did not alter the basic character and the ways of life of the people of Kashmir as these had been set before their arrival.

As elsewhere in India, in Kashmir also the Brahmans occupied the most privileged and honoured position. A vast majority of them were engaged in the study of scriptures and the calling of priests and teachers. Besides sacrificial fees and gifts of all sorts, the main source of their income was the revenue derived from the *Agraharas* or land grants donated by the kings and other man of means. The life of the bulk of the Brahmans was thus such that it involved little manual work. As such, they wielded considerable influence in the society. Brahmans had relations with kings. On the day of coronation of the, the priest had to perform special sacrifices, reciting *mantaras* meant for the attainment of the long life, fearlessness, prosperity and the like. The Bahamans according to *Nilamatapurana* clearly indicate that Brahmans had to specialize in Vedic studies.

One of the most note worthy features of early Kashmir society was that women had access to good and liberal education. In Kashmir, the status of a woman was much better than in the rest of India. Here they were afforded opportunity to distinguish themselves in any sphere of social activity. As a matter of fact "They had emerged from the domestic into the political stage, were free, owned landed and other immovable property, managed their own estates and even fought on the battle field as generals and commanders at the head of troops several women have played a significant rolc in shaping the political history of Kashmir. We know that Sugandha, Didda, Srilekgh, Suryamati, Anangalekha, Jayamati and Kalhanika played an important role not only in politics but in the field of administration also. Some of these queens were also engaged in the works of social welfare. In this region Nona proved to be a good diplomat. Silla and Chudda have shown their velour in military command. They proved their usefulness for their kingdoms at the time of crises. Suryamati the queen of king Ananta helped her husband to overcome his initial difficulties in administering the state. Queen Kalhanika, was sent on a delicate diplomatic mission of bringing about a rapprochement between Jayasimha and Bhoja.

On the basis of discussion made about the position of women in ancient Kashmir, we may conclude that though the women were better placed and somewhat free in comparison to their counterparts in rest of the country, by and large, they were subordinate to men and had to live according to the wishes of males. In spite of adequate freedom of movement, absence of veil for all practical purposes and active participation in politics, it is difficult to say if women were equal to men socially, economically, and legally. The traditional male dominated society still continued. As a house wife the women had to perform various duties prescribed by the *smriti*-writers. In addition, she helped the family by sharing the responsibility of males in agriculture. Even then the males exercised strict control over the women and the latter had to follow their husbands.

But the dependence of women does not mean that they were ill-treated or their contribution to the well-being of the society and the state was small, or they had no personality of their own. They were honoured and respected in all stages of their life. In fact, they were very valuable to man folk and the society in general. May be, on statute books they did not have equal legal rights with males, but they were not killed for dowry and were not violated as in present days. They were never punished with the sentence of death. They were the acknowledged authority on customs and traditions and they were consulted as such. They were far better in status than their contemporary women in other countries of the world.

Because of liberal education and a congenial atmosphere, the women in Kashmir took keen interest in the affairs and of the state. Many of them were successful rulers. They inherited property and managed it in their own right. They fought battles and worked for the religious and cultural promotion of their state. History of ancient Kashmir is not complete without women's contribution.

The class of prostitutes, known from early times, existed as a distinct social unit in the period under review. They are called *vesyas, ganikas, varangana's, rupajiva's* and *abhisarikas* in ancient Indian literature. These terms are indicative of their different categories. *Matsya Purana* lays down a list of their different categories. *Matsya Purana* lays down a list of their duties and rights as well as the special clauses of law applicable to them. *Kuttnimatam* gives a vivid description of the life of a *ganika* during the period the institution of prostitutes was well established as a normal feature of the society. They were protected by the state. Courtesans not only made the city attractive but also adorned the royal courts by their presence.

The institution of *Devadasi* also existed. They were known as *Devadasis* because, through their art and skill, they served the god or Deva. They could not marry and were expected to spend their whole life in the service of the gods to whose temples they were attached, but later they entertained the priests and royalty.

The courtesans were to be well versed in dancing and singing and were to give dance performances on auspicious occasions. Though as artists they were respected yet as women their status was low. The courtesans and *devedasis* could not be accepted as wives and society would not accept them as its honourable citizens.

Kashmir's reputation as the cradle of knowledge finds a special mention not only in the indigenous Sanskrit and Persian literature but also in the accounts of the foreign scholars and travellers. The Chinese pilgrim Hiuen Tsang during visit to the valley was highly impressed by the talent and scholarship of the Kashmir's and he writes that "they love learning and are well instructed." The great indologist of the eleventh century, Abu Raihan al-Biruni, while highlighting the pre-eminence of Kashmir in knowledge and erudition, says Kashmir along with Varanasi was a great centre of Hindu learning and knowledge during his time. This tradition continued till as late as the sixteenth century as we find the students of the neighbouring countries flocking there to learn and acquire knowledge at the feet of Kashmiri scholars. In fact, Kashmir is the only region in the Indian subcontinent which can claim the distinction of possessing an uninterrupted series of records of records of its history and culture.

Kashmir remained under the yoke of Hindu and Buddhist rulers till the 14th century A.D. under these kings the various sects of Hinduism(Shavism, Vishnuism and Tantracism) and various forms of Buddhism(Mahayana and Vijrayana) got impetus to rise and flourish together and peacefully. The Kings gave patronage by donating temples in honour of particular deity or by building *Stupas* as well as by granting *agraharas* for the maintenance of the Buddhist *Viharas* and the *mathas*. Donation of temples and *stupas* were also made by the queens and the ministers of the king.

Kashmir has been a meeting place of different nations. North of it is Tibet, and to its north-east is the Russian and Chinese Turkistan. Due to its geographical situation it was in the ancient and middle ages a commercial centre between India and central Asia. A large number of coins found here bear a testimony to this fact. Despite the difficulty of its route through Kashghar, the wandering pilgrim monks took the philosophical ideas beyond its borders and attracted foreign pilgrims and students to Kashmir and subsequently to India. Yuan-Chwang is right in saying that "Kashmir is one of the most important and most famous lands in the spread and development of Buddhism.

According to a version Buddhism, had led the country of Kashmir in awakening the common people and arousing a spirit of defiance in the against obscurantism and social injustice. A dynamic society of freedom had taken birth which was absorbed in making original contribution to philosophy, literature, arts, architecture and science. From here spread Buddhism beyond Himalayan countries. Its wandering monks took philosophical ideas beyond its borders to Ladakh, Tibet, Khotan, china, etc. All these are indebted to Kashmir for Buddhism, Buddhist literature and civilization.

In Kashmir, the Shaiv Agamas were accepted as revelation and became the basis of all religious thought in the Shiva community about the middle of the ninth century, two other terms, *Trika* and *Pratyabhijna* are frequently used to describe Kashmir Shavism. It is called *Trika,* because it deals with three principles, Shiva, Sakti, Anu, or Pati, Pasa, Pasu. It is also called *Pratyabhijna,* because according to it release of the individual soul depends on the recognition (*Pratyabhijna*) of its identity with Shiva. The ontology of Kashmir Shavism is predominantly monistic in nature, which may have resulted from the influence of the teachings of Sankara in this region.

Side by with Buddhism and Shavism, the cult of vaishnuism also flourished in Kashmir during the Hindu period. In the Vaishnuism of Kashmir we find a synthesis of the different Vaishnuva cults which were current in ancient India. It seems to have mingled the faith of the Vedic Vishnu, the system of Pancharatra School the religion of the Satavata and the faith of the cowherd god Gopala Krishna. In Kashmir different forms (avtaras) of Vishnu came to be worshiped. Of all the incarnations, Varaha(boar), Krishna(cowherd boy) and Narasimha (man lion) were made popular.

Bibliography

Primary Sources

1. *Abhidhanappadipika*, Moggallana Thero. Government Printer, Ceylon. 1900, 3rd Ed.
2. *Abhidharmakosa*, Acharya Vasubandhu, Ed. by Shri Rahul Sankrityane, Kashi Vidyapitha, Banras. 1988 B.S.
3. *A Catalogue of the Chinese Translation of the Buddhist Tripitaka*, the Sacred Canon,Vunyiu Nanjio Oxford Clarende Press 1976-83, M.Dece. LXXXIII.
4. *Adhayavajra Sangraha*, Ed. By Bhattacharya, Gaekwads Oriental Series, N.XL. Orient Institute, Baroda. 1972.
5. *Agam Shastra Vivranam* (Mandukya Karika Bhasyam) Shankaracharym, Raghunath Pathshala Library, Jammu (Ms.).
6. *Ain-i-Akbari*,Vol.I, Tr, by H.Biochman. 1873, revised by Sri Jadunath Sarkar.
7. *Ain-Akbari*, Vol. II, TR. by H.S. Jarret, 1891, revised by Shri Jadunath Sarkar.
8. *Ain-i-Akbari*, Vol. III, J.N. Sarkar.
9. *Ancient India* (Described in Classical Literatue Greeks and Latin Texts), J.W. Mcrindle, Wesr Minister, 1901.
10. *Anguttara Nikaya*, Ed. Pali Tex Society, 1885-1900.
11. *Aryamanjusrimulakalpa* (Ed. By Mahamahopadhyaya T. Gan Pati Sastri) Part I, II, III, Trivandrum Sanskrit Series No. LXX, 1920.
12. *Asokavadana* (The legends of Emperor Ashka in Indian and Chinese Texts) Tr. by Dilip Kumar Biswas. Calcutta, 1967.
13. *Aslasahsrika Projnaparamita*, Tr. by Edward Conze. The Asiatic Society, Calcutta, Dec. 1958.

14. *Astadhyayi* by Panini Acharaya, Lakshmivenketshar, Steem Press, Bombay. Samwat 1935.
15. *Atharva Ved*, Tr. by Damodar Satvalekar, Vols, I,II,III, 1st Edition, Sitara, 1929.
16. *Avadan Kalpalata* of Kesmendra, Ed. By Sarat Chandra Dass, Calcutta, 1888.
17. *Avadan Kalpalata*, Ksemendra, Mani Churamani Avadan, Tr. by Devi Datta Pandey, Allahabad, 1907.
18. *Babar-Nama* or *Tuzuki-i-Babari*, Tr. by A.S. Beveridge, Vols, I,II and III; Luzac & co., London, 1921.
19. *Bhavani Sakatr-Stuli*,Pt. Kesav bhatta, Srinagar, Ed. II.
20. *Braham Sutra Vedanta* Darshanam, Badrayana, Asiatic Society of Bengal, Bapist Mission Press, Vol. I, Calcutta 1863.
21. *Brihat-Katha-Manjari*, Ksemendra, Niraya SagarPress, Bombay 1931. (Kavyamala Series).
22. *Brihatkatha-Sarat-Sagar*, Ksemendra, Nirnaya Sagar Press,Bombay (Kavyamala Series).
23. *Buddhist Legends or Dhammapada*, Tr. by Watson Burlingame, Part I and II Harward University Press, 1921.
24. *Buddh-Cheritam*, Asvaghosa, Sanskrit Bhavan, Bihar. 1953.
25. The Record of Buddhist Religion as practised in India and Malaya Archipelago by I-Tsing Tr. by J. Takakasu, Oxford. 1896.
26. *Buddh-Bani*, Ed. & Tr. by Viyogi Hari, Sasta Sahita Mandal, Delhi. 1935.
27. *Charucharya*, Ksemendra, (Raghunath Pathshala Library, Jammu, Ms.)
28. *Culavamsa* (more recent part of Mahavamsa) Tr. By Wilhelm Geiger in Ger., and by Mrs. Mabel Rockmers in English. Ceylon Government information Department. 1953.
29. *Dashavatar Charitam*, Ksemendra, Niraya Sagar Press, 1930 (Kavyamala Series).

30. *Dathavamsa*, Tr. by Bimal Churan Law, Moti Lal Benarsi Dass, Lahore, 1925.

31. *Desopdesha and Narmamala*, Research Department Kashmir State, Arya Bhushan Press, Poona, 1924. (Kashmir Series No. 40).

32. *Dhammapadam*, Tr. by Shri Rahul Sankrityayane Prayag, 1933, edition I (Mahabodhi Granthmala-I).

33. *Dhavanyaloka*, Abhinavagupta, Ed. By Dr. Nagendra, Delhi 1952. Edition 1.

34. *Digha-Nikaya*, Pali Text Society, 1890-1911. Tr. by Sacred Books of the Buddhists II-IV; 1899-1951 by Frank Gottingen. 1913.

35. *Dipvamasa*, Tr. by Hermann Oldenberg, William & Norgate, London and Edinburgh, 1879.

36. *Dipvamasa*, Edited by Dr. B.C. Law. July 1957.(The Ceylon Historical Jounal).

37. *Notes on Diplawansa*, Part I, Ghose,Katyayani Press, Calcutta, 1916.

38. *Divyavadan*, Ed. By E.B. Cowell and R.A. Neil, Cambridge University Press, 1996.

39. *Do-Ka-Zang* (A brief Summary), Hon'ble Sir Charllas Elliott, Publ. as supplementary paper to Buddhist Text Society of India, Darjeeling, 1895.

40. *Edicts of Asoka*, Tr. by G. Srinivas Murti, A.N. Krishna Ayangar, R.V. Rama Swamy Ayangar.

41. *Epigraphic India*, Vol. IX. July 1908 and Vol. XVIII, 1925-26.

42. *Fo-She-Hing-Tsan-king* (A life of Buddha) by Asvagosha Boddhisattva, Dharmaraksha A.D. 420, from Chinese into English by Samuel Beal (Sacred Books of the East Vol. XIX) Oxford, 1883.

43. *Gaschte Des Buddhismus In Indian*, Taranatha, Tr. in Ger. By Von Anton Schiefner S. Pettersburg, 1869.

44. *Gilgit Manuscripts* Vols. I,II & III, Ed. By Nalinksha. Dutt, Pub. By Maharaja Hari Singh, Srinagar, Kashmir, 1939.

45. *Inscriptions of Kambuja*, R.C. Majumdar, Calcutta, 1939.

46. *Isvara-Pratyabhijna Vimarshini of Utpaladeva, with a Vimarshani by Abhinavagupta,* Ed. By Pt. Mukund Ram Shastri, Vol. I and II, Nirnaya Sagar Press, Bombay, 1918 (Kashmir Series).
47. *Jataka Tales,* Vols. I,II, III and IV (Hindi) Tr. by Anand Kauslyan, Hindi Sahitya Sammelan, Prayag, 1956.
48. *Jatakattthakatha,* Bharatiya Jnanapitha, Kasi 1951.
49. *Jehanjir's Inida* pf Francisco Pelsaert, Ed. By W.H. Moreland & P.Goyel, Cambridge, 1925.
50. *Kapphinabhudaya of Siva Svamin,* Ed. By Gauri Shankar, Lahore, 1937.
51. *Kathasarat Sagar, Ocean of Stories,* Tr. by Sri. N.M. Richard Penzer, Printed in Great Britain, Vols. I-X.
52. *Kathasarat Sagar by Somdeva Bhatta,* Ed. By Pandit Pundurang Parab, 'Nirnaya Sagara' Press, Bombay 1889.
53. *Kathavathhu,* Ed. by Arnold.C. Taylor, Pub. By the Pali Text Society by Henry Frowde, London, 1897.
54. *Kathavathhu,* (Pointsof Controversy or subject of Discourse) Tr. of Kathavathhu from the Abhidharma Pitaka by Shwe Zan Aung & Mrs. Rhys Davids. Pub. By the Pali Text Society, London 1915.
55. *Khuddaka Patha,* A Pali Text with a Translation & Notes by R.C. Childers.
56. *Kulacudamani Nigama,* Ed. By Arthur Avalon with an introduction by Aksaya Kumar Maitra, Publishers and Co., Madras. 1956.
57. *Kuttanimatam Kavyam,* Damodar Gupta, Tr. by Jagan Nath Pathak, Mitra Prakashan, Allahabad.
58. *Lalitavistara* . Ed. By Heransgegeben Von. & Dr. S. Lefmann, Halle. A.S. 1902.
59. *Lalitavastara,* Tr. by Rajendra Mitra, Asiatic Society of Bengal, New Series No. 455 Calcutta 1881.
60. Lankavatara *Sutra,* Tr. by Daisetz Teitaro Suzuki, Routledge and Kegan Paul Ltd., London, 1956.
61. *Mahayanavimsaka of Nagarjuna,* Ed. By Vidhusekha Bhattacharya, Calcutta, April 1931.

62. *Mhaabharta*, Ed. & Pub. By Manmath Nath Dutt., M.A., M.R.A.S., Elysium Press Chandra Ray, Calcutta, 1895.
63. *Mahabharta*, Tr. by Pratapa Chandra Ray, Calcutta, 1888.
64. *Mahavagga (The Vinaya Pitaka)*, Ed. By N.K. Bhagwant Bombay University Publication, Bombay 1944.
65. *Mahavamsa of Dharmapala*, Tr. in Hindi by Anand Kauslyan, Hindi Sahitya Sammelan, Prayag, Sm. 2014 or 1960.
66. *Mahavastu Auadan*, A' L' imprimere Nationle, Paris, 1882.
67. *Majjhima Nikaya*, Ed. Pali Text Society, 1888-1902.
68. *Malti Madhava of Mahakavi Bhavbhuti*, Chowkhamba Sanskrit Series, Banaras, 1954.
69. *Mataya Purana*, Calcutta, 1876.
70. *Memoirs of Babar*, Tr. by John Leyden Esq. and William Friskine, Universitp Press, Oxford, 1921.
71. *Milindapauho*, V.Trenckner, The Royal Asiatic Society, London, 1928.
72. *Milindapanho*, Pali Text in Devnagari Edition by R.D. Vedekar, Pub. by the University of Bombay, 1940.
73. *Milindapsnho, (The questions of King Milinda)* Tr. from the Pali by T.W. Rhys Davids. The clarenden Press, Oxford, 1890 (Sacred Books of the Easr Vol. XXXV).
74. *Mcrindle's Ancient India, as described by Ptolemy*, Ed.by Surender Nath Majumdar Sastri, M.A., Calcutta. 19927.
75. *Mulamadhyamakakarikas* Ed. Poussin Biblothica Buddhica, 1913.
76. *Mohenjadaro and Indus Civilization*, Vol. III, Sir John Marshall, 41, Great Russel Street, London, 1931;
77. *Nilamat or Teachings of Nila*, Ed. By K. Vreese, Ph.D., Leiden, E.J. Brill, 1936.
78. *Nilamatapuranam* Ed. By Ram Lal & Pt. Jagaddhar Zadoo, Lahore. 1924.
79. *Ouchltya-Vlchar-Charcha* by Ksemendra Kavyamala Series, a Bombay.
80. *Padam Purana*, Poona 1893.

81. *Pag Sam Jon Zang (History of the rise, Progress and fall of Buddhism in India)* Ed. By Sarat Chander Dass, Calcutta 1908.
82. *Puggalapannati*, Ed. Pali Text Society, 1883.
83. *Rajatarangini* by Kalhana, Ed. By Stein, M.A., I & II. Vols. Westminister, 1900.
84. *Rajatarangini of Kalhana*, Jonaraja, Shuka & Prajgsbhatta, I, II & III Vols. by Jogesh Chandar Dutt. Calcutta Publication 1898.
85. *Ramayana*, Nirnaya Sagar Press, Bombay 1810.
86. *Rigved*, (Hindi Tr.) Indian Press, Prayag 1954.
87. *Rudrobhasyam* by New Shankracharya, Bani Vilas Press, Rungnagar, 1913.
88. *Samyamatrika, Ksemendra*, Kavyamala Series, Bombay, 1925.
89. *Samyutta-Nikaya*, Part I Ed. By Leon Peer, and.
90. *Samhutta-Nikaya*, Part II Ed. by Leon Peer, Pub. For the Pali Text Society, London, 1884, respy.
91. *Sarva-Darsana of Sayna Madhava* Ed. by Mahamahopadhyaya Vasudeva Shastri Abhyankar Pub. by Bhandarkar Oriental Research Institute, Poona, 1924.
92. *Sasnavamsa*, Tr. by Bimal Churu Law Luzac & Co., London, England, 1952.
93. *Saundarnanda*, Asvaghosha, Biblotheca Indica, Work No. 192.
94. *Saundarnandam, Asvaghosha* Tr. by Suraya Narayan Chowdhary.
95. *Saundarnanda Kavya, Asvaghosha*, Ed. by Har Parsad Shastri, Calcutta, 1939 (R.A.S.)
96. *Shankar Digvijy*, Ed. by Hari Narayan Apte. 1915.
97. *Shivsutra, Vimarshini The Sutra of Vasugupta* Vol. I, Commentary by Ksemraja Srinagar. 1911 (Kashmir, Series).
98. *Shiv Sutra-Vartikam, Varadaraja*, Ed. by M. Kaul, Srinagar Samest 1909 (Kashmir Series No. 43).

99. *Sragdhara-Stotram, Bhikshusarvajna Mitra of Kashmir*, Ed. by Satish Chandar Vidya Bhushan, Calcutta, 1908.

100. *Sumangalavilasini* I. Ed. Pali Text Society, 1886.

101. *Tattvasangraha of Santaraksita with a commentary of Kamalasila*, Ed. and Intro. By Ember Krishnamacharya, Vols. I & II Central Library Baroda,

102. *The Bhilsa Topes, Brev. Major Alaxandar Cunningham*, Smith Elder & Co. London 1854.

103. *The coins of Ancient India*, Major General Sir A. Cunningham, London. 1891.

104. *The Greeks in Bactara &India*, W.W. Tarn, Cambridge University Press 1951.

105. *The History of Buddhism, Bu-Ston*, Parts I & II Tr. from Tibetan by Dr. E. Obermiller, Heidlberg. 1932.

106. *The Legends of the Topes, Thupvamsa*, Tr. In English by B.C. Law, Published by R.A.S.B. Calcutta, 1945.

107. *The Mahavamsa*, Tr. in English by Wilhelm Geiger, Assisted by Mabel Haynes Bode, Ph. D., Published for the Pali Text Society 1912.

108. *The Mongol Empire,* Michael Prawdin. Tr. by Eden and Ceder Paul, George Allen. A Unwin Ltd.

109. *The Saddharma Pundrika*, Tr. ny Kern, The Clarenden Press Oxford, 1909. (The Sacred Books of the East Vol. XXI).

110. *Tibetan Tales,* Tr. from the Tibetan of Kah-gyur by F.Anton Von Schiefner, done into English by W.R.S. Rolston, London, Kegan Paul, Trench, Trubnor and Co. 1906.

111. *Udanvarga,* a collection of verses from Buddhist Canon compiled by Dharmatrata, being the Northern Buddhist version of Dhammapada, Tr. from the Tibetan of Bkah-hggur by W.Woodville Rockhill, London Trubner & Co. Ludgate Bill. 1883.

112. Uttar Ram Charitam, Bhavbhuti by Sri Shesh Raj Sharma, Banaras.1949.

113. *Voyu Purana*, Poona 1893.

114. *Vastu-Sastra*. Vol. II, Bhartiya Vastu-Sastra Series, Vol. IX; Dr. D.N. Shukla, Gorakhpur.

115. *Vinaya Pitakam*, Ed. by Hermann Oldenberg, William and Norgate London and Edinburgh, 1879-80, 81 (I,II & III volumes).

116. *Vikramakdev-Charitam, Bilhana*, Raghunath Pathshala Library Ms.

117. *Vikramnakdev-Charitam by Bilhana*, I Bhapter, Sanskrit Granthmala. Banaras, 1954.

118. *Verses of Nur-ud-Din Rishi* and the Lyrics of Habba Khatun, J.L. Kaul.

A. **Travels**

1. *Albiruni's India*, I & II Vols., Dr. Edward C. Sachan, London, Trubner & Co. Ludgate Hill, 1888.
2. *A Journey form Bengal to England*, George Forester, London, 1808.
3. *Journey to Lhasa and Central Tibet*, Sarat Chandra Das, Ed. by Hon. W.W. Rockhil, 2nd Edition London, 1902.
4. *Notes on Our-Kong' Account of Kacmer* by M.A. Stein. Wein, 1896.
5. *On Yuan Chwang Travels in India*, 629-645 Thomas Watters, Vol. I and II, Ed. after his Death by T.W. Rhys Davids, London 1904.
6. *Si-yu-ki Hioun-Thsang* Vol. II Samuel Beal (1958 Sushil Gupta) Calcutta.
7. *Travels in Laddkh and Kashmir,* Willaim Moorcraft and Mr. George Frebed, I and II Vols. London.
8. *Travels in India and Kashmir*, Erich Von Schonberg, Vol. II, Hurst and Blackett Publishers, 1857.
9. *Travels in Kashmir and Punjab*, (Tr. from Ger.), Baron Charlas Hugel, London, 1845.
10. *Travels in the Mughal Empire*, A.D. 1656-1668, Francis Bernier, West Minister.
11. *Travels in Kashmir Ladakh and Iskardu*, G.R. Vigine, I and II Vols. London. 1841.
12. *Travels of Fahein and Sun-Yun*, Buddhist Pilgrims From China to India 400 A.D. and 518 A.D Tr. by Samuel Beal, Trubner and Co. London, 1869.

13. *The Pilgrimage of Fa-hein (From the French Edition of Foe-Koucki)*, Remusat, Klaproth and Landresse, Calcutta, 1848.
14. *The Charms of Kashmir*, V.C. Scott, O'Conner, Longmans Green & Co. London, New York, Bombay, Calcutta, Madras. 1920.
15. *The Record of Buddhist Kingdoms. The Chinese Monk Fa-hein*, James Legge. Oxford. 1886.
16. *The travels of Fa-hein* 399-414 A.D. H.A Giles.
17. *YatraKe Panne* (Hindi) by Rahul Sankrityayane, Sahitya Sadan, Dehra Dun. 1952.
18. *The Travels of Marco Polo* London, III, Publication 1950.

Secondary Sources

Agarwal, R.C., *Kashmir and its Monumental Glory*, New Delhi, 1998.

Ahmad, Iqbal, *Kashmir under Hindu Rajas*, Srinagar, 2007.

Allen, G.F., A Buddha's philosophy, London, 1959.

Collett, John. A guide for visitors to Kashmir, Calcutta, 1884.

Altekar, A,S., Education in Ancient India, Varanasi, 1951.

Altekar, A.S., State *and Government in Ancient India*, Delhi, 1984.

Altekar, A.S., *Position of Women in Hindu Civilization*, Banaras, 1956.

Ayer, K.B., Art and Thought, London, 1947.

Bader, (Miss) C., Women in Ancient India, London, 1925.

Bamzai, P.N.K., *Culture and Political History of Kashmir*, Vol.- I, New Delhi, 1994.

Bandyopadhaya, N.C., *Economic Life and Progress in Ancient India*, Allahabad, 1980.

Banerjee, G., The Hindu law of marriage and Satridhana, Calcutta, 1923.

Basham, A.L., The wonder that was India, picador, 2004.

Bates, C.E., *A Gazetteer of Kashmir*, Delhi, 1980.

Bazaz, P.N., *Daughters of Vitasta*, Delhi, 1959.

Beal, S., Life of the Hiuen Tsang, Kegan paul, 1911.

Beal, S., *Si-Yu-Ki.* (Tr), *Buddhist Records of Western World*, Vol. II, New Delhi, 1970.

Bhandarkar, R. G., Vaisnavism, Saivism and minor religious sects, Strasburg, 1913.

Bhandarkar, R.G., *Collected works*, Poona, 1928.

Brown, Percy., Indian Architecture(Buddhist and Hin), Bombay, 1959.

Brown, Persy, *Indian Architecture* (*Buddhist and Hindu Period*), Calcutta, 1959.

Brown, Persy, *Indian Architecture* (*Islamic Period*), *Calcutta*, 1942.

Chanana, Dev Raj., *Slavery in Ancient India*, Delhi, 1960.

Chandra, M., *Trade and trade Routes in Ancient India*, Delhi, 1979.

Chatterji, J. C., Kashmir Shavism, Srinagar, 1914.

Chaudhari, J.B., *The Contribution of Women to Sanskrit literature*, vol- i& ii, Calcutta, 1939-1941.

Cirmack, Margaret., *The Hindu Women*, N.Y. 1961.

Conze, Edward, Buddhism, oxford, 1957.

Cunningham, A., *Coins of Medieval India*, Delhi, 1967.

Cunningham, Sir Alexander, *Coins of Medieval India from the Seventh Century Down to the Muhammadan Conquest*, Varanasi, 1967.

D avids, T.W. Rhys, Buddhism, London, 1917.

Das, R.M., *Women in Manu and His Seven Commentators*, Varanasi, 1962.

Das, S.K., The education system of the Hindus, Calcutta, 1930.

Desai, Kumud., *Indian law of Mirage and Divorce*, Bombay, 1963

Dhar, Somnath, *Tales of Kashmir*, New Delhi, 1992.

Dutt, J.C., *Kings of Kashmir* (*Tran's. Of Kalhana's, Jonaraja and Srivaras Rajatarangini-3 Vols*), Calcutta, 1887.

Dutt, Nalinakaksh, Early Monastic Buddhism, Calcutta, 1914.

Elliot & Dawson, *The History of India*, vol- ii, Allahabad, 1963.

Elliot, C., Dowson, J., History of India as told by its own historians, London, 1867.

Fabric, C., A History of Indian Dress, oriental Longman, 1960.

Ganhar. J.N., Buddhism in Kashmir and Ladakh, Delhi, 1956.

Ghosal, U.N., Hindu revenue system, 1929.

Ghoshal, U.N., *Economic Condition*, Bombay, 1966.

Ghure, G.S., Indian Costumes, Bombay, 1951.

Ghurey, G.S., *Caste and Class in India*, Bombay, 1957.

Ghurey,G.S., *Social Tensions in India*, Bombay,1968.

Gopal, Lallanji., The Economic Life of Northern India, Varanasi, 1965.

Hasan, Mohib-Bul, Kashmir under sultans Calcutta, 1959.

Hussain, Majid, *Systematic Geography of Jammu and Kashmir*, New Delhi, 2000.

Inrda, *The Status of women in ancient India*, Banaras, 1955.

Jamwal, Suman, *Economy of Early Kashmir*, Jammu, 1994.

Jayal, Shakambhari, *Status of Women in the Epics*, Delhi, 1995.

Jolly, J., *Hindu law and Custom*, Calcutta,1952.

Jolly, J., Hindu Law and Customs, Calcutta, 1982.

Kak, R.C., Handbook of the Archaeological section of the Sri Pratap Singh Museum, Srinagar, Calcutta, 1923.

Kak, R.C., *Ancient Monuments of Kashmir*, New Delhi, 1987.

Kane, P.V., *History of Dharmasastra*, vol- ii, poona,1944.

Kapur, M.L., *Kingdom of Kashmir*, Srinagar, 2005.

Kapur, M.L., *Studies in History and Culture of Kashmir*, Jammu, 1976.

Karve, Irawati., *Hindu society- an interpretation*, Poona 1961.

Kaul, G.L. Kashmir through Ages, Srinagar, 1954.

Kaul, Pandit Anand, Jammu and Kashmir state. Calcutta, 1913.

Keith, A.B., History of Sanskrit Drama oxford University press London, 1954.

Khan, A.R., *Geography of Jammu and Kashmir*, Srinagar, 2007.

Knowles, B. Rev, J. Hinton, Dictionary of Kashmiri Proverbs and Sayings, Bombay. 1885.

Knowles, B. Rev, J. Hinton., Folk Tales of Kashmir, 1893.

Koul, A., *Ancient Savants of Kashmir*, Delhi, 1987.

Krader, L., People of Central Asia, Netherland, 1963.

Lal, p., *Sanskrit love lyrics*, Calcutta, 1966.

Landis, G. Mary., *Reading in Marriage and the Family*, New Jersey, 1952.

Law, Bimal Churan., Ancient Indian Tribes, Lahore, 1926.

Law, Bimal churan., Buddhist Studies, Calcutta and Simla, 1931.

Lawrence, W.R., *The Valley of Kashmir,* Srinagar, 2006.

Luckvinder, Sing Sodhi, S., *The History of Ancient Kashmir*, Srinagar, 2006.

Majumdar, R.C & Madhavandana .,*The Great Women f India*, Almora,1953.

Mancini, J.G., *Prostitutions and Their Parasites* trans. By D.G. Thomas, London, 1963.

Maneek. B. Pithawalla, An introduction to Kashmir, its Geology and geography, oxford university press, 1953.

Max, Muller., *The Laws of Manu in Sacred Books of The East*, Vol- xxxv, Delhi, 1964.

Mees, G.H., *Dharma and society*, London, 1935.

Mitra, Veda. *Happy Married Life in, Ancient India,* Delhi, 1964.

Mitter, Dwarka Nath., *The Position of Women in Hindu Law*, Calcutta, 1913.

Mookerji, R. K., Culture and art of India, Delhi, 1959.

Mujamdar, B.P., *The Socio-Economic History of Northern India*, 1960.

Mujamdar, R.C., Age *of Imperial Kannauj*, Bombay, 1965.

Mujamdar, R.C., *Ancient India*, Delhi, 1980.

Mujamdar, R.C., *Classical Age*, Bombay, 1956.

Mukerjee, Radha Kamal, cosmic Art of India, Bombay 1965.

Mukerjee, Radha Kamal., Mirrors of Indian culture Delhi, 1982.

Myer, J.I., *Sexual Life in Ancient India*, London, 1930.

Nila, *The Nilmatpurana*, Vol. II, *A Critical Edition and English Translation by V. Kumari*, J & K Academy of Art, Culture and Languages, Srinagar, 1973.

Niyogi, P., Contribution to the Economic History of Northern India, Calcutta, 1962.

Om Prakash, Food and Drink in Ancient India, Delhi, 1961.

Panday, Kanti Chandra., Abhinava-Gupta an historical and philosophical study, Banaras, 1959.

Petech, Luciano, A study on the chronicles of Ladakh, Calcutta. 1939.

Prakash, O., Food and drink in ancient India, Delhi, 1961.

Prasad, B., *Theory of Government in Ancient India*, Allahabad, 1927.

Prince, James., Essays on Indian Antiquities Vol. I, London, 1858.

Puri, B.N., *India in Classical Greek Writings*, Ahmadabad, 1963.

Puri, B.N., *India under Kushanas*, Bombay, 1965.

Qadri Shafi Ahmad, *Biscoe in Kashmir*, Srinagar, 2000.

Rabbani, G.M., *Ancient Kashmir a Historical Perspective*, Srinagar, 2009.

Rabbani, G.N., *Kashmir Social and Cultural History*, Srinagar, 2007.

Ray, H. C., Dynastic History of Northern India, Calcutta, 1931

Ray, S.C., *Early History and Culture of Kashmir*, Srinagar, 2008

Rice, Stanley, Hindu Customs and their Origin, London, 1937.

Rookh lalla, The charms of Kashmir, London, 1854.

Ross, Alieen. D., *The Hindu Family in Urban Setting*, Oxford, 1961.

Saividian, K.G., *Education, Culture and the Social order*, Bombay 1963.

Sastri, A.M., *India as Seen in the Kuttnimatam of Damodaragupta*, Delhi 1975.

Saxena, S.K., *Political History of Kashmir*, New Delhi,1974.

Sengupta, Nilkashi., Evolution *of Hindu Mirage*, Bombay, 1965.

Shali, S.L., *Kashmir History and Archaeology Through Ages*, New Delhi, 1993.

Sharma, R.S., *perspective in Social and Economic History of Early India*, Delhi, 1983.

Sharma, B.N., *Social Life in Northern India*, Delhi, 1966.

Sharma, R.S., *Perspective in Social and Economic History of Early India*, Delhi, 1983.

Shastri, A.M., *India as Seen in the Kuttanimata of Damodragupta*, Delhi, 1975.

Shastri, Shakuntala Rao., *Women in Sacred Laws*, Bombay, 1953.

Shastri. D.R., *The Origin and Development of the Rituals of Ancestor Worship in India*, Calcutta, 1963.

Sicar, D.C., *Studies in the Society and Administration of Ancient and Medieval India*, Calcutta, 1967.

Singh, Y.B., Social Life in Ancient India, New Delhi, 1981.

Singh, Y.B., *Commercial Activity in Ancient Kashmir, in the Proceedings of the Punjab History Conference*, Tenth Session, 1976.

Singh, Y.B., *Kashmir and Nepal, in the Proceedings of the Punjab History Conference*, Fourteenth Session, 1980.

Singh, Y.B., *Religious Significance of Designs on Early Indian Coins, in the Proceedings of Tenth International Congress of Numismatics*, London, 1966.

Sircar. D.C., *Some Aspects of the Earliest Social History of India*, London, 1928.

Sircar, D.C., *Indian Epigraphy*, Delhi, 1965.

Sircar, D.C., *Social Life in Ancient India*, Calcutta, 1965.

Sircar, D.C., *Studies in the Society and Administration of Ancient and Medieval India*, Vol. I, Calcutta, 1967.

Smith, V.A., *Early History of India*, Oxford, 1924.

Stain, M.A., *Kalhana's Rajatarangini, Chronicle of the Kings of Kashmir*, Vols. I & II, Delhi, (Reprint), 2007.

Stein, M.A., Memories on the Ancient Geography of Kashmir, Calcutta, 1889.

Sufi, G.M.D., Kashir., Lahore 1948.

Thakur, Upender., *The History of Suicide in India, Delhi*, 1963.

Thomas . P., *Indian Women through the Ages*, Bombay, 1964.

Thomas, P., *Hindu Religion, Customs and Manner*, Bombay, 1963.

Thurston, E., *Cast and Tribes in Southern India*, Madras, 1909.

Tripathi . G.M., *Marriage Forms under Ancient Hindu law*, Bombay, 1906.

Tripathi, R.S., *History of Kannauj*, Banaras, 1937.

Upadhyaya, V., Socio-Religious conditions of north India, Varanasi, 1964.

Vaidya, C.V., *History of Medieval Hindu India*, Vol. I, Poona, 1921.

Venkatesvara, S.V., Indian culture through the ages, London, 1928.

Warmington, E.H., *The Commerce Between Roman Empire and India*, Delhi, 1974.

Watters, Thomas, *On Yuan Chang's Travels in India*, Vols. I and II, (Ed) T.W.R. Davidas, London, 1904.

Wilson, H.H., *The Hindu History of Kashmir*, Srinagar, 2006.

Wilson, H.H., *The Visnu-Purana, A System of Hindu Mythology and Tradition*, Calcutta, 1961.

Yadava, B.N.S., Society and Culture in Northern India, Allahabad, 1937.

Yaday, B.N.S., *Society and Culture in Northern India in the 12th Century A.D.*, Allahabad. 1973.

Index